BEYOND COURAGE

Members of a Zionist youth group pose in the formation of a Star of David, Yugoslavia, ca. 1927–1933

BEYOND COURAGE

The Untold Story of Jewish Resistance During the Holocaust

Doreen Rappaport

CANDLEWICK PRESS

Photography and art credits appear on page 222.

Pages 1 and 196: "I am a Jew and will be a Jew forever," by Franta Bass, reprinted from *I Never Saw Another Butterfly: Children's Drawings and Poems from Terezin Concentration Camp, 1942–1944*, edited by Hana Volaková (Prague: Jewish Museum; New York: Schocken, 1993), copyright © by Židovské Muzeum v Praze (The Jewish Museum in Prague), by permission of the family of Franta Bass.

Pages 17 and 167: "While you have breath," by Abraham Sutzkever, and "The Partisan Song," words by Hirsch Glick, music by Dmitri Pokrass, both reprinted from *The Last Lullaby: Poetry from the Holocaust*, edited by Aaron Kramer (Syracuse, NY: Syracuse University Press, 1999), copyright © by the Dora Teitelboim Center for Yiddish Culture, by permission of the Dora Teitelboim Center for Yiddish Culture/Center for Cultural Preservation, www.yiddishculture.org.

Page 46: "I will betray tomorrow, not today," by Marianne Cohn, reprinted from *Jewish Resistance in France, 1940–1944*, by Anny Latour (New York, Holocaust Library, 1981), first published in French as *Résistance juive en France, 1940–1944* (Paris: Éditions Stock, 1970), copyright © by Éditions Stock.

Page 59: "Broken people," by Zdeněk Weinberger, reprinted from *We Are Children Just the Same: Vedem, the Secret Magazine by the Boys of Terezín*, by Marie Rút Křížková, Kurt Jiří Koutouč, and Zdeněk Ornest, translated by Elizabeth Novak and edited by Paul Wilson, by permission of the University of Nebraska Press. Copyright © 1995 by Aventinum, Prague. English-language edition copyright © 1995 by the Jewish Publication Society.

Page 82: Portion of "The Little Smuggler," by Henryka Lazowertówna, reprinted from *The Warsaw Ghetto: A Guide to the Perished City* by Barbara Engelking-Boni and Jacek Leociak, translated by Emma Harns, copyright © Yale University Press, by permission of Yale University Press.

Page 107: Portion of "The Song of the Slaves of Leptocaria," by Maurice Chaim, reprinted from *The Illusion of Safety: The Story of the Greek Jews During the Second World War* by Michael Matsas (New York: Pella, 1997).

First edition 2012

Library of Congress Cataloging-in-Publication Data

Rappaport, Doreen.
Beyond courage : the untold story of Jewish resistance during the Holocaust. — 1st ed.
p.   cm.
ISBN 978-0-7636-2976-2
1. World War, 1939–1945 — Jews — Rescue — Juvenile literature. 2. World War, 1939–1945 — Jewish resistance — Juvenile literature. 3. Righteous Gentiles in the Holocaust — Juvenile literature. 4. Holocaust, Jewish (1939–1945) — Juvenile literature.   I. Title.
D804.6.R37 2012
940.53'18 — dc23   2011048116

LEO 17 16 15 14 13 12
10 9 8 7 6 5 4 3 2 1

Printed in Heshan, Guangdong, China

This book was typeset in Adobe Jenson Pro.

Candlewick Press
99 Dover Street
Somerville, Massachusetts 02144

visit us at www.candlewick.com

For Jack Kagan, who shared his journey.

For Bob Rosegarten, who shared this journey.

In memory of my father, Meyer Rappaport,

who launched my journeys.

CONTENTS

Background image:
Prayer books and religious texts damaged by arson during *Kristallnacht,* 1938

PART FOUR: IN THE CAMPS

"During the cold nights" 107

◾

Background image:
Barracks at Kaufering IV labor camp, Hurlach, Germany

PART FIVE: PARTISAN WARFARE

"This song was written with our blood, and not with lead"   167

∎

∎

"I am a Jew and will be a Jew forever"   196

Introduction

All of the remarkable stories you will read in this book are true, and are about real people — Jews who were part of a network of resistance throughout German-occupied Europe during the Shoah (Holocaust). Some of these resisters were teenagers or young adults, but they took on the mantle of adult responsibilities and committed themselves to rescuing others. Many died in their efforts. Those who survived went on after liberation to rebuild their lives. I am filled with admiration when I think of the strength it must have taken to start over — after having lost so many loved ones — and the courage it must have required to risk loving and experiencing joy again.

When I started researching this book, the only examples I knew of Jewish resistance came from popular books and movies, and were limited to the Warsaw Ghetto Uprising and the escape from the Sobibor death camp. And still I did not know the real or complete stories behind those two extraordinary events. Even as a Jew, growing up in a Jewish household, I had only ever heard that "Jews went like lambs to the slaughter" during the war. Researching this book, I learned that the truth was quite different. From the beginning of Hitler's ascent in Germany and all through the war, Jews resisted the Nazis with uprisings and escapes and rebellions. But resistance is not defined just by dramatic, militant events like these.

Jews refused to renounce their religion and celebrated their holidays in secret, improvising essential ritual objects. They set up secret schools, giving their children hope for the future. They collected diaries, testimonies, art, and photographs so the rest of the world would have a record of what had happened. They became expert forgers, providing other Jews with new identification and ration cards so they would not starve. They devised ingenious plans to smuggle children out of danger, to find hiding places for them, and to take them across mountains and through barbed wire to safe countries. Perhaps Eta Wrobel, a Jewish partisan, said it best: "The biggest resistance we could have done to the Germans was to have survived."

For six years, I have lived with the people you will meet in this book. I've gotten to know most of them through the words and photographs they left behind. I have had the privilege of speaking directly with survivors, and I have even had the good fortune of meeting a few in person. All are enshrined in my heart. Writing this introduction is the final piece of the book, but it has proven to be the most difficult. It is a good-bye, and I do not want to let go. The scope and extent of Jewish resistance during the Holocaust cannot possibly be contained in one book. These people and their stories are a seed inside me that keeps growing. Therefore, I will continue my journey by adding other resistance stories to my website.

I hope you will consider this book a first step in your own journey of exploration and discovery, and I invite you to continue traveling with me at www.doreenrappaport.com.

Doreen Rappaport

PART ONE
THE REALIZATION

I am a Jew and will be a Jew forever.
Even if I should die from hunger,
never will I submit.
I will always fight for my people,
on my honor.
I will never be ashamed of them,
I give my word.

I am proud of my people,
how dignified they are.
Even though I am suppressed,
I will always come back to life.

— Franta Bass, Theresienstadt ghetto, German-occupied Czechoslovakia,

age eleven, ca. 1942–1944

Nazi election propaganda postcard, 1932

HITLER IN POWER
Germany, 1933–1938

The nightmare that turned into the Holocaust began in Germany. Under Adolf Hitler's rule, the Nazis initiated the Final Solution, a policy aimed at the annihilation of all Jewish men, women, and children in Europe. Under this policy, the Germans and their Axis partners caused the deaths of as many as six million Jews. They also killed 220,000 Roma and Sinti (Gypsies), 200,000 people with disabilities, 15,000 homosexuals, and millions of other innocent civilians.

Adolf Hitler came into power as chancellor of Germany on January 30, 1933, during a worldwide depression. Five million Germans were out of work; they were frightened, confused, humiliated, and still bitter over their country's defeat in World War I, fifteen years before. Germany had been made to sign the Treaty of Versailles, which forced it to give up some of its territory, limit its army, and pay huge reparations for war damages. Hitler, the *Führer* (leader), played on people's confusion and distress and spouted his racial theory that Aryans — by which he meant people of Nordic descent — were a superior race to all others. He predicted that Germany would rise again as a world power. Germans, including children, embraced his words with wild enthusiasm. His words gave them new hope and pride.

Hitler's campaign to destroy all political opposition moved with lightning speed. He banned all political demonstrations except those of his party, the National Socialists, or Nazis. Dachau, the first concentration camp, was opened in March 1933, and more than forty-eight hundred Social Democrats, communists, trade unionists, and other political opponents were imprisoned there.

At the same time, Hitler began his fanatical campaign against the Jews. Anti-Semitism had a long, ugly history in Europe and met with willing ears in Germany and in most

Background image: Members of the League of German Girls wave Nazi flags, Vienna, Austria, March 1938

2

European countries. Jews had suffered persecution for over two thousand years just for being Jews. They were blamed for Jesus's death. Some people believed that Jews killed Christian children and then used the blood to make matzos for Passover seders. Thousands of Jews were murdered during the Crusades in the eleventh and twelfth centuries. They were blamed for the Black Death (the plague) in the fourteenth century. During the Spanish Inquisition, Jews were expelled from Spain and Portugal or burned at the stake. In some countries, Jews were forced to live in walled-in sections of cities called ghettos. In the 1880s and early twentieth century, thousands were murdered in Russia and Poland in organized mass violence, known as pogroms.

A German sign reads, "Jews not wanted here."

Hitler played on these long-standing prejudices against Jews and blamed them for all of Germany's problems, even though Jews were only one percent of the population. Through an insidious propaganda campaign using radios, newspapers, billboards, posters, exhibits, and even children's books, ugly stereotypes about Jews were reinforced and absorbed by a prejudiced populace. New laws called the Nuremburg Laws stripped Jews of their citizenship, and other laws destroyed their educational and economic opportunities. Jews were forced to sell their businesses to Aryans for a fraction of their worth. They were banned from civil service jobs and careers in journalism, art, literature, broadcasting, and theater. Jewish doctors could not practice medicine at government hospitals. The list of professions barred to Jews made it impossible to support one's family. Jewish children were no longer permitted to attend German public schools or universities. At first, the Nazi strategy was to eliminate the Jews, not yet by murder but by forced emigration.

Despite the persecution and hatred, German Jews believed they would survive this nightmare. But on November 9 and 10, 1938, the persecution turned to organized violence and shattered any illusions Jews had that they could accommodate to life under Adolf Hitler.

Hitler on the campaign trail

The Turning Point

November 10, 1938, started out like any other school day for sixteen-year-old Ernst Günter Fontheim. The morning was gray and chilly, not unusual for this time of year. He walked the five hundred yards from his apartment house to the train station, took the elevated train six stops, then walked a short block to his school.

Ernst Günter Fontheim, 1938

As he did every day, he went straight to his classroom, expecting to see his teacher, but Dr. Siegfried Wollheim wasn't there. In fact, none of the teachers were in their classrooms. One of the students said the teachers were having a special meeting in the teachers' conference room. Ernst listened as some of his friends reported what they had seen that morning on their way to school: people running and shouting through the streets and dark clouds of smoke curling up into the air. Some boys, whose routes took them through commercial sections of Berlin, reported seeing mobs smashing signs and windows of Jewish-owned shops and department stores. Glass was shattered all over the sidewalks and into the gutter. The vandals ran into the stores shouting anti-Semitic slurs. When the looters emerged, weighed down with stolen dresses and shoes, they were greeted by waves of cheering. The police stood by through all this, doing nothing.

The slurs and the ugly laughter didn't surprise Ernst. In the almost six years since Hitler had come to power, boycotts against Jewish-owned stores and a never-ending string of discriminatory laws had crippled every aspect of Jewish life. But the violence did surprise him. Ernst had heard of scattered vicious assaults against Jews, but no one in his family and no one he knew had ever been attacked.

Finally Dr. Wollheim appeared. It usually took him a while to settle down his rambunctious students, but today all talking stopped as soon as he entered the room. He announced that everyone was being dismissed from school because their safety could no longer be guaranteed, and explained that it was too dangerous for them to be gathered in one place. Roving mobs were destroying Jewish property and burning synagogues all over the city. The school could be stormed at any moment. He told his students to go directly home — they shouldn't linger or visit friends. Their parents would be worried. He warned them not to walk in large groups, which were more likely to attract attention and possible violence. When would they return to school? one boy asked. Dr. Wollheim answered that they would be notified.

Ernst waited impatiently for his train. On the route home, he looked out the window at familiar sights. He saw his synagogue, a magnificent edifice topped by three cupolas. He was stunned to see a thick column

Background image:
As a synagogue burns, firefighters work instead to save a nearby house, Ober-Ramstadt, Germany, November 1938

of smoke rising out of its center cupola. The sight struck him like a lightning bolt. He completely forgot Dr. Wollheim's warnings, got off at the next stop, and raced back the few blocks to his synagogue. He had to see what was happening.

Police barricades held back a crowd shouting all-too-familiar anti-Semitic slurs. The flames shooting up from the cupola looked much larger than they had from the train. If the fire was not quenched soon, the entire synagogue would be destroyed. However, the firefighters' long hoses were blasting water not at the synagogue but at the buildings next to it, to save non-Jewish property from harm.

Ernst's thoughts were focused on the Torah scrolls, the most sacred and revered document of his people. They were enshrined in the Ark, a special cabinet, behind the *bimah*, a raised platform at the front of the sanctuary. On his bar mitzvah three years ago, he had chanted a portion of this sacred document. He was terrified by the thought that the Torah scrolls might catch fire.

Prayer books and religious texts damaged by arson during *Kristallnacht*, 1938

Someone in the mob called out that there was a Jewish family living on the ground floor of a nearby building. That announcement was followed by the noise of splintering wood, a deadly silence, then wild cries of triumph as an elderly bald man was dragged out of the building. The mob pushed him. A tall man in a long coat and a floppy hat pounded his leather briefcase over the elderly man's head like a hammer until his face was streaked with blood. Ernst was convinced the attacker belonged to the Gestapo, the German secret police, though he wore no uniform.

A new voice cried out, "How cowardly. So many against one!" The speaker repeated the phrase over and over as the crowd attacked him.

A police officer shoved the elderly Jewish man into a police car and drove off. In a daze, Ernst turned and raced back to the train station to go home.

SAVING THE SACRED TORAHS

On November 10, 1938, fourteen-year-old David Zwingermann and Horst Löwenstein sneaked into the rubble of the Temple of Peace Synagogue on Markgraf-Albrecht-Strasse in Berlin and carried twelve undamaged Torah scrolls out to safety.

For two days, Jews in every city, town, and village in Germany and Austria, which Germany had taken over earlier that year, hunkered down in their residences or in hiding, hoping to evade the mob violence. More than seventy-five hundred Jewish-owned businesses and thousands of Jewish homes were vandalized. Two hundred sixty-seven synagogues in Germany, Austria, and the Sudetenland (a largely German area of Czechoslovakia that Hitler had recently

Hechingen synagogue, Hechingen, Germany, November 12, 1938

7

claimed) were set on fire and their contents vandalized and destroyed. Jews were dragged out of their homes in their nightclothes, then taunted while their property was looted or burned. Shattered glass along with feathers ripped from blankets and pillows were strewn about the Berlin streets. Jewish men and women were forced to sweep up the debris and pay for the destruction even though they were the victims. The fine was 400 million dollars (one billion Reichsmarks). Ninety-one people were murdered. Thirty thousand Jewish men, ages sixteen to sixty, were rounded up by Hitler's special forces, the SS, and taken to concentration camps.

The Nazis called the two-day rampage *Kristallnacht*, "the Night of Broken Glass." They declared it a "spontaneous" outpouring on the

Jews rounded up during *Kristallnacht,* Buchenwald concentration camp, November 1938

RETALIATION

On October 28, 1938, Hitler expelled seventeen thousand Polish Jews living in Germany, sending them back to Poland. When the Polish government refused to take in Jews whose passports had expired, twelve thousand men, women, and children were stranded on the Polish border

Jewish deportees line up for soup, Zbaszyn, Poland

in subfreezing weather without adequate shelter or food. The parents of Herschel Grynszpan, a Polish student living in Paris, were among those expelled. They wrote him a note describing their dire situation. Grynszpan's assassination of a German diplomat was his desperate protest against the brutal treatment of his parents.

part of their followers in retaliation for the assassination of a German diplomat in Paris by Herschel Grynszpan, a seventeen-year-old Jew, on November 7. But the sanitized term did not fool German or Austrian Jews. They knew they had experienced a pogrom. Ernst's family understood all too well that there was no safety or future for them in their own country. The discriminatory, racist laws of the past six years had evolved into violence and terror that would no doubt be repeated.

Like tens of thousands of other German Jews, Ernst's father, Georg Fontheim, tried every avenue possible to get visas for his family to emigrate, but nothing came of his attempts.

Less than a year later, in September 1939, Germany attacked Poland and sparked the outbreak of World War II. The Germans drafted Jews into forced labor, mostly in defense plants to replace Aryan workers now in the army. In April 1941, Ernst was sent to the Siemens munitions factory in Berlin. Six months later, the Germans began deporting Berlin's Jews to ghettos and extermination camps. For a while Ernst thought he was safe, because Jews who worked for the war effort were exempt from deportation. But in the summer of 1942, an influx of non-Jewish workers forcibly imported from occupied France, Poland, and Czechoslovakia arrived at the Siemens factory. Ernst knew that it was only a matter of time before Jewish workers would no longer be needed.

Six months later, after his parents and sister were deported to their deaths in Auschwitz, Ernst acquired forged identification papers as an Aryan — a non-Jew — and went underground with his future wife, Margot, and her parents, and they survived the war. About fourteen hundred Jews survived the war underground in Berlin, helped by sympathetic Germans.

After *Kristallnacht*, individual solutions and help were no longer practical or possible. The number of Jews wanting to leave Germany and Austria was overwhelming. Jews needed the world community to come to their aid and help rescue them. But such a response did not occur, so Jews devised their own plans for rescuing themselves.

A Wrenching Decision

Marianne Prager stood over her father as he searched through a collection of international telephone books, which had been bought by Jewish organizations. He scoured the pages, looking for his family name in Amsterdam, Buenos Aires, and New York City, hoping to find distant relatives who might help his family immigrate.

Georg Prager, fiercely proud of his German heritage and his medal for military service in the Great War, was now a broken man. After *Kristallnacht*, he could no longer lie to himself: there was no way Jews could possibly work around the madman who ruled their country.

Sixteen-year-old Marianne did not know when the next round of violence would occur, but she knew that it would, and so did her father. He was determined to get his family out of Germany.

Legal emigration was extremely complicated, if not nearly impossible. Families needed innumerable documents signed in duplicate and triplicate by German officials. Her father needed certificates of "good conduct," proof of military service, and proof of no prison record. Bribes would inevitably have to be paid. Even if the family managed to gather

Marianne Prager (right) and her sister, Ilse Prager

the necessary documents and bribe the right people, they would leave Germany nearly penniless. Jews were prohibited from taking their money out of the country, not that the Pragers had much left to take out.

Even if a family overcame those considerable obstacles, few Western countries were willing to take in such large numbers of Jews all at once. In order to enter the United States, for example, an immigrant needed an American citizen to guarantee support if he or she should become destitute. The American Jewish Joint Distribution Committee (known as "the Joint"), a philanthropic organization, provided funds for living facilities in Switzerland for Jewish refugees.

Jewish youths leaving Berlin for Palestine, 1936

A friend helped Georg write letters in English to strangers in the United States. "Quite by chance I came into possession of your name. I think we must be related. . . ." He went on to describe his family's desperate situation, then begged for help in getting out of Germany.

Georg Prager received a few replies, but nothing concrete developed.

One evening sometime later, two Zionists from an organization called Youth Aliyah came to the Prager apartment. Zionists were Jews who dreamed of a Jewish homeland in what was then known as the British Protectorate of

Palestine. The young men explained that Youth Aliyah had been sending Jewish youth, ages ten to fifteen, to Palestine (now called Israel) since 1933. They would live there in a kibbutz, a communal settlement, where they would study Hebrew and learn the skills necessary to build the new nation. Marianne was too old to be eligible, but twelve-year-old Ilse was not. Georg Prager, however, refused to consider separating the family.

Marianne understood her father's reluctance but felt that her sister should be allowed to go. Marianne and her parents were stuck in Germany for now, their future uncertain. Expelled from public school, Marianne was studying at a Jewish school to be a governesss, a job still open to Jews. However, there was no guarantee she would even get a job.

Deprived of education, no longer allowed at concerts or theaters, and forbidden to buy newspapers, Marianne desperately needed stimulation for her active and curious mind. So she met in secret with other young people to talk politics, read and analyze forbidden books, and listen to forbidden music. How glorious it was to share ideas and to break the isolation of their lives. The meetings were a lifeline that kept them from sliding into hopelessness.

Marianne shared what she learned with Ilse, whose life was even more limited than hers. She wanted her sister to leave Germany. Ilse had a real chance for something better. In Palestine, she could help create a new and better world. She would be valued, and her talents would be fostered. If she left Germany, at least one member of the family would surely survive.

Georg Prager did not change his mind about letting Ilse go to Palestine, but he finally realized that separating the family might offer

Arrivals in Harwich, Great Britain, on a *Kindertransport* from Germany, December 12, 1938

their best — or only — hope. He wrote a letter to a cousin in London, asking if he would take Ilse in.

For five years, Jewish leaders in Great Britain had been pressing their government to take in, on a temporary basis, an unspecified number of Jewish children up to age eighteen. Finally the British government had relented, with the stipulation that the Jewish community financially support all refugees. On December 1, 1938, two hundred children, ages two to seventeen, left Germany on the first *Kindertransport* to England (*Kinder* means "children" in German).

On May 21, 1939, it was Ilse Prager's turn to join the *Kindertransport*. Georg's London cousin had agreed to take her in.

The night before Ilse left, Marianne helped pack her sister's clothes, treasured roller skates, and family mementos. Children could take only what they could carry in one small suitcase. The roller skates weighed down her case and took up a lot of space, but Ilse insisted.

A German official came to the apartment later to examine Ilse's suitcase to make sure she wasn't taking any valuables out of the country. If valuables were found in even one child's case after they boarded the train, the whole *Kindertransport* could be turned back to Germany.

Marianne pressed a leather diary into her sister's hands. Knowing how frightened Ilse must be, leaving her family, Marianne urged her to write in the diary every day. The writing would make it seem like they were having a conversation. She made Ilse promise not to "shed one tear" when it was time to leave.

Hundreds of children, some as young as six months old, were at the railroad station, ID tags pinned to their jackets. Starting in January 1940, all Jews whose given names did not correspond to a Nazi list of authorized Jewish names would have *Sara* printed as their middle name if female, *Israel* if male. Passports of all Jews would be stamped with a red *J* on the front, making it easy for the Nazis to identify Jews.

Passport of Gertrud Gerda Levy, evacuated from Germany on a *Kindertransport* to Great Britain, August 23, 1939

Parents and children clutched one another as they said their good-byes. Some children sobbed quietly, while others screamed. Ilse managed to hold back tears until her father broke down. Georg was grateful to the English for taking in Jewish children. Still, he was sending his twelve-year-old daughter off to a strange country where she did not speak the language or understand its traditions or foods, to live with people she barely knew. And he didn't know when or if he would ever see her again.

Despite her instruction to Ilse, Marianne cried, too.

Ilse Prager was one of ten thousand Jewish children from Germany, Austria, Czechoslovakia, and Poland sent to England, Holland, and Sweden on the *Kindertransports*. From 1933 to 1945, Youth Aliyah sent fifteen thousand Jewish youths to Palestine from Germany, Austria, Czechoslovakia, Poland, Romania, and Holland.

A bill was introduced in the U.S. Congress to admit twenty thousand refugee children from Nazi Germany into the country, but it failed to pass. Why? Because it was feared that when those children grew up, they might take jobs from Americans.

Like Ilse Prager, most children never saw their parents again.

A WAY OUT

In 1932, several young men visited Recha Freier, a social worker and the wife of a rabbi in Berlin. The men were convinced that they had been fired from their jobs because they were Jews. Freier immediately saw an answer to their problem and the problems of other unemployed Jewish youths: emigration to Palestine. Surrounded by Jews striving to build

Loading hay at the Hachshara farm, Gut Winkel, Germany, ca. 1935–1936

a nation, the young could find a purpose for their lives no longer available in Germany. As the Nazi persecution escalated, Youth Aliyah — Aliyah meaning "ascent to the land of Israel" — expanded its purpose to rescue Jewish youths. Many would prepare for life in Palestine by first living in communal settlements in Germany, Austria, and Holland.

PART TWO
SAVING THE FUTURE

While you have breath
I too exist —
as the pit of the plum
contains what will come:
tree, nest, robin
and all the rest.

— Abraham Sutzkever, Vilna ghetto,

age twenty-nine, 1942

HITLER'S CAMPAIGN FOR WORLD DOMINATION

Simultaneous with his methodical degradation of Jewish life, Hitler shaped his campaign for world domination. Defying the Treaty of Versailles, he rebuilt Germany's armed forces and, in 1936, sent thirty thousand troops to take back the Rhineland, one of Germany's former territories, from France. He insisted that he needed *Lebensraum*, "living space," for his people. The world community did not stop his aggression, and his grabs for territory continued for six years.

On March 13, 1938, Germany incorporated Austria as part of the Nazi plan to unify all persons deemed to be German into a single state. That same year he insisted that Czechoslovakia's Sudetenland, where three million people of German descent lived, rightfully belonged to Austria and therefore now belonged to Germany. He promised that this would be his last territorial demand. France and Britain, unwilling to go to war over Hitler's invasion, signed an agreement in September allowing the annexation. Czechoslovakian officials were not invited to the conference that sealed their people's fate.

Europe at the height of Nazi power, 1942

Greater Germany and its occupied territories

German allies or dependent states

N   0   200 mi
     0   200 km

Finland
Norway
Sweden   *Baltic Sea*
Estonia
Great Britain   *North Sea*
Ireland
East Prussia   Latvia
Denmark
Danzig   Lithuania
Netherlands
Belgium
Germany
Poland   Soviet Union
Occupied Northern France
Luxembourg   Bohemia-Moravia   Slovak Republic
Switzerland   Austria
Vichy France   Hungary   Bessarabia
Romania
Spain
Corsica   Italy   Yugoslavia   *Black Sea*
Bulgaria
Sardinia   Albania
Turkey
Greece
Sicily
AFRICA   *Mediterranean Sea*

With original 1938 borders shown

Six months later, in March 1939, Hitler broke his promise by marching his troops into the protectorate of Bohemia-Moravia, thereby securing total control of Czech territory. Slovakia was separated from Czechoslovakia and became an ally and puppet state of Nazi Germany.

In August 1939, Germany and the Soviet Union signed a nonaggression treaty renouncing war against each other. In September, Germany attacked and conquered Poland from the west, and shortly afterward, the Soviet Union attacked and conquered it from the east. According to the secret part of their agreement, Poland was split: the Soviets occupied eastern Poland, while Germany occupied western Poland.

But Hitler was still not satisfied. In 1940, he invaded and conquered Denmark, Norway, France, Holland, Belgium, and Luxembourg. In April 1941, German forces occupied Greece and Yugoslavia. By then, the countries of eastern Europe had joined Italy and Germany in what was being called the Axis. In June 1941, Hitler betrayed his pact with the Soviets and attacked the Soviet Union. By 1942, most of Europe was held or led by Germany or pro-Nazi regimes.

In the Loborgrod concentration camp, Yugoslavia (now Croatia), 1941

A Star of David badge marked with *Jude,* the German word for Jew

Throughout German-occupied cities and ghettos in Europe, excepting Denmark, as well as in concentration camps, the Nazis forced Jews to wear identifying badges displaying the Star of David. The star, usually outlined in black, had the word *Jew* printed in the center in mock Hebraic style. Most often the star was printed on coarse yellow cloth. In the Warsaw ghetto, Jews wore a white armband with a blue Star of David. This Nazi perversion of the Jewish Star of David was a visible form of humiliation and discrimination, making it simple to identify Jews.

A Star of David stamped with *Juif,* the French word for Jew

19

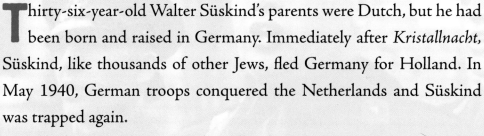

Coffee and Tea

AMSTERDAM, THE OCCUPIED NETHERLANDS

Walter Süskind

Thirty-six-year-old Walter Süskind's parents were Dutch, but he had been born and raised in Germany. Immediately after *Kristallnacht*, Süskind, like thousands of other Jews, fled Germany for Holland. In May 1940, German troops conquered the Netherlands and Süskind was trapped again.

Life for Jews in occupied Holland turned out even worse than Süskind had feared. In an effort to win over the Dutch people, the Nazis at first pretended to be friendly occupiers. Their real intentions became clear, however, when they instituted the same anti-Jewish policies they had imposed on Germany.

The Nazis discovered willing allies in the Dutch Nationalist Party (NSB), and anti-Semitism among the party's ranks quickly exploded. NSB followers harassed and beat up Jews and destroyed Jewish stores in Amsterdam. When the Dutch police force turned a blind eye, Jewish youths took matters into their own hands and formed a defense group. On Tuesday, February 11, 1941, aided by sympathetic non-Jews, the group attacked NSB members. In the wake of that attack, sixteen Jewish men were arrested, interrogated, and tortured. The next day the Nazis used the incident, which they termed a riot, as justification for closing off a section of Amsterdam heavily populated by Jews.

Süskind saw signs go up, proclaiming that section "a Jewish district." On the doors and windows of his favorite restaurants were notices forbidding Jews from entering or dining.

Background image:
Pro-Nazi Dutch Nationalists march
at a rally, Amsterdam, 1940

20

Ten days later, another violent clash occurred in Amsterdam. This time more than 389 Jewish men were arrested and sent to concentration camps. Horrified by the attack on its Jewish population, Amsterdam's citizens called a general strike that spread to other cities. The Nazis squelched it in three days.

As they did in all occupied countries, the Nazis appointed a "Jewish council" of prominent Jews, purportedly to run the day-to-day affairs of the Jewish community. Süskind knew that in reality, the councils had little or no authority. They were Nazi tools that confronted Jews with an impossible dilemma: carrying out Nazi policies against their own people. Council leaders tried to negotiate with German authorities to help their people. Most attempts failed. Some council members believed that by

A confrontation with NSB members, Amsterdam, the Netherlands, February 11, 1941

serving the Nazis, they might at least save their own lives and the lives of their families. SS Commander Ferdinand aus der Fünten appointed Walter Süskind to the council. Süskind himself had a wife and child. Nevertheless, he vowed to use his position to help other Jews in whatever way he could.

In June 1942, the Nazis ordered the council to draw up lists of Jews in Amsterdam to be sent to work in labor camps in Germany. The sophisticated Nazi propaganda machine constantly created language to deceive the Jews. When the Nazis stated that Jews would be "resettled" in the East or in "labor camps," most Jews believed their lies. They did not know they were being sent to concentration camps and that they faced

Deportation center at the Hollandsche Schouwburg Theatre, Amsterdam, the Netherlands

almost certain death on arrival. In June 1942, Walter Süskind might not yet have realized that most deportees were being sent to their deaths, but he understood how difficult life in the camps would be and that many people would not survive.

The council sent out notices to four thousand young people, but fewer than two thousand showed up. Thousands went into hiding and, in spite of nightly house searches and raids, only five hundred were rounded up.

Commander aus der Fünten created a temporary deportation center for Jews in Amsterdam's Hollandsche Schouwburg Theatre and put Süskind in charge of the center. Paintings and sculptures adorning the lobby were taken out. Carpets were pulled up. The cushioned seats were unbolted from the floor and stacked against the walls. Guards were stationed day and night outside the front entrance.

Some weeks as many as one thousand adults lived crowded together in the theater, some on the balcony floor, others in theater boxes, some on the stage. Mattresses were given to elderly women, but most adults slept on their coats, flea-ridden horse blankets, or straw. There were only two men's toilets, three women's toilets, and a few sinks. In warm weather, the stench inside was overwhelming. People were allowed out of the theater for only one hour a day to walk in the courtyard.

Children younger than thirteen were taken from their parents and housed in a day-care center across the street. In keeping with the Nazi regulation that forbade Jews and Christians to work together or socialize, the entire day-care staff was Jewish. Only its sixty-four-year-old director, Henriëtte Pimentel, was not. A devoted, compassionate administrator, Pimentel instructed her staff

Deportees in the courtyard of the Hollandsche Schouwburg Theatre, summer 1942

to give loving care to the children. The children's hair was brushed twice a day to ward off lice. The youngsters were allowed to run about in the back garden. As often as possible, the caretakers took the babies and

Henriëtte Pimentel with children rescued and hidden by the Dutch underground

Jewish children brought from the day-care center to a children's home by the Dutch underground

toddlers to the theater to be fed by their mothers.

The names and vital statistics of all Jews were noted on file cards. The Germans checked the list to make sure that parents and children were deported together. While Süskind knew it would be impossible to save most adults, he believed he might save children and was determined to save as many as possible. He walked across the street to the day-care center and asked Henriëtte Pimentel if she would help. She agreed immediately.

Süskind made contact with the Dutch underground student groups that were placing Jewish children with Christian families in the countryside. He would telephone activists Joop Woortman and Piet Meerburg and tell them he had a package of coffee or tea for them. "Coffee" referred to a child with dark skin and dark hair. "Tea" referred to a blond child. Most of the homes found for the children were far from Amsterdam, where German occupation forces were thin.

The "messengers" picking up the children were most often young women. The Germans usually stopped Dutch men and examined

Jewish child-care workers take children for a stroll, Amsterdam, the Netherlands

their identity cards to make sure that they weren't supposed to be working in factories in Germany. When women were stopped and questioned, it seemed natural that they were out with their own children or with younger sisters and brothers.

Süskind learned the schedule of the streetcars that stopped in front of the day-care center. At the precise moment that a tram blocked the view of the guards in front of the theater, a messenger would leave the day-care center with a "bundle" and hop on a streetcar. It was easiest to smuggle out babies and small children. They were often given a drop of wine to make them drowsy and then hidden in suitcases, backpacks, laundry baskets, or sacks of potatoes. After a while, most tram conductors guessed at the contents of the bundles, but they never said anything. Their silence also saved lives.

The bundle was taken to a safe house. One safe house was in the storeroom of a secondhand clothing store, where new clothes were provided. Then it was off by train or bicycle to the countryside with identity documents for the now "Christian" child, forged by Süskind's coworker Felix Halverstad and his team.

As children disappeared, Halverstad destroyed the registry and file cards with their names, passports, and food-ration cards and doctored the card index to match the number of children remaining in the day-care center. Sometimes parents who were being deported were given pillows wrapped in blankets, made to look like swaddled babies, to disguise the fact that their children had been rescued. When they were marched off into vans, the parents talked to and caressed these fake baby bundles.

As the deportations were stepped up, Süskind turned to Johan van

Hulst, director of the neighboring Protestant Teachers College, for additional help. Hulst had seen the lines of Jews being herded into vans and knew what the Nazis had in store for them. An additional escape scenario was invented: A young child was taken into the back of the college. Only one building and a few shrubs separated the college from day-care center in the rear. Once inside, Hulst waited with the child by the front door. A messenger then rang the bell and was let in. The messenger gathered up a bundle while Hulst stood watch at the window. When the tram stopped in front of the college and the coast was clear, the messenger jumped onto the streetcar or walked casually down the street, taking the bundle to a safe refuge.

Older children could not be smuggled out in bundles and backpacks, so Süskind managed to convince aus der Fünten that they should be allowed out with their caretakers for short walks around the neighborhood. What aus der Fünten never realized was that the walks, too, were timed to coincide with the streetcar schedules. Twenty-five children went out for walks; only twenty-three returned.

But it wasn't just the forging or the clever escape strategies that were crucial. Süskind had to keep aus der Fünten ignorant about what was going on. He set out to ingratiate himself with the commander and spent many an evening drinking gin with him. Having been born and educated in Germany, he spoke German fluently and understood the German mind and temperament. Aus der Fünten enjoyed Süskind's company: "the Jew" told a good story

Dutch forgers at work

and had a big repertoire of German songs. As the singing became more raucous, Felix Halverstad, working quietly in his office downstairs, rearranged the file cards to make children disappear. Süskind was aware that most Jews did not understand why he was so friendly with a Nazi and even believed that he was a collaborator. Nevertheless, he kept up the pretense because it was essential to the success of the rescue operation.

In September 1943, Süskind learned that all children still at the day-care center would be deported, and he organized a final push to smuggle out as many more as possible. The center was closed for good on September 29, 1943, one day before Rosh Hashanah, the Jewish New Year. All remaining council members and their families were deported to the Bergen-Belsen concentration camp. The Dutch underground offered to hide Süskind, but he would not abandon his people

The deportation of Amsterdam's Jews, June–September 1943

Walter Süskind and his daughter

or separate from his family, and chose to be deported with his wife and five-year-old daughter. None of them survived the war.

The Dutch smuggling network hid a total of 4,500 children, 385 of them from the day-care center. Most survived the war, but only 1,417 children found their parents alive afterward. The Hollandsche Schouwburg Theatre is now a memorial to the Jews sent to their deaths from this site.

MIRJAM WATERMAN

MENACHEM PINKHOF

JOACHIM SIMON

JOOP WESTERWEEL

THE YOUNG ZIONISTS

Mirjam Waterman, Menachem Pinkhof, and Joachim Simon worked with Joop Westerweel, a non-Jew, to save the lives of more than 320 young Zionists living in Holland. They found hiding places for some in Holland and smuggled others out of the country into France, where they found their way through Spain to Palestine. Waterman and Pinkhof were betrayed and sent to Bergen-Belsen but survived the camp and later married. They emigrated to Palestine in 1946. Simon and Westerweel lost their lives saving others.

Members of Youth Aliyah plant a garden, the Netherlands

No More Saras

Respectable Christian names, Joseph and Yvonne, had replaced Hertz and Hava Jospa's real first names on their forged identity cards. Deportations had started in Belgium in the summer of 1942. Seventeen thousand foreign-born Jews had been rounded up in one hundred days and shipped off to Poland. The Jospas, originally from Bessarabia, were vulnerable. No one was certain what had happened to the deportees, so the National Front of Belgian Independence sent a university student to Poland to find out. Victor Martin traveled to the region near the Auschwitz concentration camp and reported back: "People are being burned." On learning this, Jewish women in Brussels immediately mobilized to save Jewish children.

Hertz and Hava Jospa

The Jospas hid in the apartment of a Christian friend in Brussels. But even if the Germans found them, at least their young son, Paul, would now be safe: friends had taken him in. Separating from Paul had been excruciating. It was too risky even to visit him. Their friends would sometimes notify them when they were taking Paul for a walk, and then Hertz and Hava would watch their precious child from a distance.

Hava knew that most Jews were not as lucky as they

The Anciaux family with Annie and Charles Klein (on laps), whom they sheltered during the war, Brussels, Belgium, ca. 1943–1945

Andrée Geulen

were — with friends who were willing to risk their own lives taking in Jewish children — so she and Hertz created the underground organization the Jewish Defense Committee (CDJ). As part of its work, the CDJ organized a secret network of Christian families and institutions willing to shelter Jewish children.

Though Belgium's constitution forbade racial or religious discrimination, most Belgian bishops and cardinals had been silent about the persecutions. Parish priests and nuns needed permission from their superiors to help, but some did not wait for permission. Hava and two non-Jews, Brigitte Moons and Yvonne Nevejean, did not hesitate to approach Catholic convents, rest homes, and schools to help. Once a safe place had been found, Paule Renard, Claire Murdoch, and Andrée Geulen were assigned the delicate job of convincing parents to give up their children, and then served as couriers, delivering the children to their hiding places. Renard was studying to be a social worker, Murdoch was already a social worker, and Geulen was an elementary-school teacher. None of the three was Jewish. Women who didn't look Jewish could travel about more freely and were less likely to be stopped and questioned. But it was still dangerous work. If discovered, these women could be sent to prison or labor camps. Men, if stopped, were often examined to see if they were circumcised, which would identify them as Jewish.

Separation was traumatic for both parents and children. Parents were being asked to turn their children over to strangers who were not even Jewish. The women couriers did not tell the parents their real names.

They did not tell them where they were taking their children. Many parents feared that their children, if placed in Christian institutions, would be converted. It was not an unreasonable fear; conversions did happen. Couriers also knew that if the parents found out the names of the foster parents, they would try to visit them and put the children, themselves, and the foster parents in danger. They tried to calm par-

Jewish girls at their First Communion, Convent of Saint Antoine de Padua, outside Brussels, Belgium

ents by promising to visit the children frequently. Some lucky parents were allowed to visit their children occasionally. Many of the older children understood that being separated from their parents might save their lives. But younger children often felt abandoned. They did not understand that it was because their parents loved them so much that they could "give them away" so that they might live.

The CDJ's extensive and efficient forging unit produced documents and food-ration cards identifying the children as Christians. There were no more Saras, only Simones. No more Israels, only Maurices. No more Herschels, only Henris. The couriers rehearsed the children over and over

Belgian resisters on an outing with a hidden child, twenty-month-old Myriam Frydland

with their new names and backgrounds. But no amount of rehearsing guaranteed that children might not accidentally reveal who they really were. Once when a passenger on a train asked a six-year-old girl her name, the child turned to Andrée Geulen and said, "What do I tell her, my real name or my new one?"

Parents who could afford it paid the host family or institution for their children's upkeep. Most often, expenses were paid by the London-based Belgian government-in-exile and the American Jewish Joint Distribution Committee. For security, the couriers were never told where the funds came from.

Ester Heiber kept track of some of the hidden children. She devised an intricate code requiring five separate notebooks. In one notebook, she listed the child's real name and a code number. In a second book, she wrote the child's false name, actual birth date, and the code number. In a third notebook, she wrote the code numbers in numerical order and the child's original address. A fourth book listed the hiding places, which had their own code numbers. The fifth notebook listed the false names alongside the codes of the hiding places. She hid the five notebooks in five separate places. Only by comparing all five notebooks

Convent nurses with Jewish children hidden by the CDJ, Belgium could anyone decipher this information. Andrée Geulen kept her own secret notebooks.

For the most part, children hidden in institutions did not venture out; a Nazi collaborator might see them and report where they were hiding.

The morning of May 20, 1943, a Gestapo officer, an interpreter, and "Big Jacques," a Jew who was a known informer, appeared at the Convent of the Nursing Sisters of the Blessed Sacred Heart in Brussels. Nine months earlier, its mother superior, Sister Marie-Aurélie, had received permission from her bishop to take in fifteen girls, ages twenty months to twelve years.

The nuns of the Nursing Sisters of the Blessed Sacred Heart, where fifteen Jewish girls were sheltered, Anderlecht, Brussels, Belgium, 1943

She had also received permission to lie if necessary to protect the children.

The Gestapo officer said he knew of the hidden girls and demanded that the mother superior turn them over. He assured her that they just wanted to reunite the children with their families. She knew different. Her only hope was to stall him until she could get someone to take the girls away. He demanded to know the children's names and that she turn over their food-ration cards. She lied and told him she did not know where all the children were. She insisted that she needed time to pack their belongings and prepare them for leaving. Her ploy worked; the Gestapo gave her until the following morning.

Sister Marie-Aurélie did not tell the other nuns what was going on. Instead she alerted Father Jan Bruylandts, a nearby parish priest, who was hiding several Jewish boys. Bernard Fenerberg, who was with the priest then, immediately went to alert Paul Halter, a member of the Belgian Partisan Army, to rescue the girls.

Halter waited for nightfall, then went to the convent with three Jewish compatriots — Bernard Fenerberg, Tobie Cymberknopf, and Jankeil Parancevitch — and two non-Jewish members of the Belgian resistance — Floris Desmedt and Andreé Ermel. Sister Marie-Aurélie at first insisted that Halter and his comrades shoot and wound her before they leave so the Gestapo would be fooled into thinking that she

Yad Vashem

Yad Vashem in Jerusalem, Israel, a living memorial to the Holocaust, encompasses a museum and a research and educational center. It also honors non-Jews who risked their lives to save Jews. Sister Marie-Aurélie, Andrée Geulen Herscovici, and Paule Renard have been honored there as Righteous Gentiles among the Nations.

Path of the Righteous at Yad Vashem, Jerusalem, Israel

had tried to stop the "kidnappers." Halter assured her that he would solve that problem some other way. But first he had to take the girls away and hide them.

When Halter returned, he cut the telephone wires, overturned desks, gagged the nuns, and tied them to chairs. A half hour after the mock kidnapping, one of the nuns "managed" to reach the window and call out to a passerby, who called the Belgian police. Sister Marie-Aurélie told her cover story: six strangers had burst into the convent, tied them up, and kidnapped fifteen girls. The police questioned them for hours, taking down all the details, but they did not alert the Gestapo until morning.

The next morning, the SS interrogated the mother superior. She described the supposed kidnapping in great detail — how these men cut the phone wires, bound and gagged her and the other sisters, and took the children away.

"Did they seem a little Jewish?"

"No, not at all. As a matter of fact, they spoke a very pure French, but they didn't say much. The one who was guarding me didn't say a single word."

"Were all of them armed?"

"Yes, all of them."

"And you didn't scream for help at all?"

"Scream? We didn't dare. They said they'd shoot us if we called out for help."

"When did you first call out, then?"

"When they left and we heard nothing."

Unable to disprove her story, the Gestapo left.

The following month, the Gestapo arrested Paul Halter and deported him to Auschwitz, where he worked in a coal mine until the camp was liberated on January 27, 1945. Forty-eight years later, in 1991, at the first Hidden Children Reunion in New York, he was reunited with several of the girls he rescued and learned that all fifteen had survived.

The Jewish Defense Committee saved more than three thousand children.

Bernard Fenerberg (second from left), Paul Halter (third from left), and Tobie Cymberknopf (fourth from left) with individuals they helped hide during the war, 1995

The Most Important Game

Every other day for six weeks, thirty-three-year-old Georges Loinger had picked up groups of children in Aix-les-Bains, a town in the foothills of the French Alps, and taken them by train sixty miles away to the small village of Annemasse, where he would smuggle them across the border to Switzerland. For their own safety, the children were not told where they were going. Nor were they told Loinger's real name.

Right from the beginning of the German occupation in France, various Jewish organizations sprang up to rescue Jewish children, many of whom were foreign-born. At first the children were put in group homes near Paris. There they continued their educations, enjoyed the companionship of other children, and had fun. Loinger, a teacher of physical education, had organized the sports programs in the homes and trained teachers.

In 1940, when Germany invaded France, the children were evacuated farther south, to the so-called free or unoccupied zone of France. The "free" zone was not under direct German military control, but it was headed by a collaborationist French government, centered in the city of Vichy, that mirrored and implemented Nazi policies.

Georges Loinger presenting awards to the monitors of the training center at Gournay-sur-Marne, Seine-Saint-Denis, France

At the Château de la Guette,
ca. 1939–1940

By 1942, there were fourteen hundred children sheltered in fourteen homes. But there was no safety there, either. Children often found themselves moved from group home to group home, or from group home to convents or to willing families. A few lucky ones got passage to the United States.

Now, in 1943, the deportations were being stepped up. The group homes were closed. Getting the children out of France was a matter of life or death. Loinger was part of a vast underground network hiding children and smuggling them out of the country. Members of *Eclaireurs*

At the Chabannes children's
home, August 1, 1942

Israelites de France (IEF), a French-Jewish scouting group; *La Sixième*; and the *Mouvement de Jeunesse Sioniste* (MJS, or Young Zionists) worked with the Society for Assistance to Children (OSE) to rescue children.

The rescue network approached non-Jewish families and non-Jewish institutions to take in children. But not all children could be so easily hidden within France. The foreign-born children, if they spoke French at all, spoke it with a distinct accent. It would be especially hard for them to pass for Christian in small villages or convents. Loinger, working for the OSE, was smuggling these children out of the country to neutral Switzerland.

It pained him to think about how much these children had already suffered. Their once-secure lives had vanished. Forced to leave their families, their homes, and their countries, they were surrounded by an unfamiliar language and unfamiliar food. Their clothing and small suitcases had been searched, all traces of their previous lives — family photographs, class notebooks, and prayer books — removed. Unable to understand why they were being separated from their parents, the little ones

Documents forged by Gilbert Leidervarger and David Donoff

cried and clung to those last tangible connections with their families. Childhood, which should have been so joyous, had turned into one frightening experience after another.

Loinger's group of fifty on this particular day was larger than usual. In the children's pockets were forged identity papers and food-ration cards. Loinger was not worried about those papers being spotted as fake. The Jewish Scouts had become expert forgers. But traveling by public transportation was fraught with danger. The Germans had recently taken over from the French police and were arresting Jews at railroad stations. Sometimes trains were stopped and German officers went from passenger to passenger demanding to see identity cards. The children had been carefully rehearsed to know their new names and the names of their new parents and new grandparents, but they were only children. A casual question could trip them up. Some of Loinger's charges looked Semitic: their facial features, hair, and skin color easily identified them as Jews.

This day was unfolding to be more harrowing than usual. Fifty German soldiers were waiting on the platform for the same train. In their excitement about traveling on a train, some children forgot Loinger's instructions to be quiet and sedate. They ran through the cars, playing tag. Loinger settled those he could into seats and then hastened to find the twenty or so still up and about. To his horror, he found them in a compartment seated on the laps of German soldiers. Enchanted by the children, the Germans were feeding them candy and chocolates. Loinger was dumbfounded

"Who are they?" a soldier asked him.

He repeated his cover story as casually as he could. "They are from

Marseilles." From January 22 to 24, 1943, the Nazis and twelve thousand French police had gone door-to-door in the Old Port of Marseilles. The Nazis considered its winding, narrow streets and alleys perfect hiding places for the enemy. The French police rounded up two thousand Jews and then dynamited fifteen hundred buildings. The bombings had devastated the children's homes, Loinger said. He was taking them to a camp to recuperate. As nonchalantly as he could, Loinger gathered the children and led them out of the soldiers' compartment. A few soldiers, enamored of the youngsters, followed him. Loinger watched fearfully as they played with the children for the rest of the train ride.

His next challenge was to get past the police patrols at the Annemasse railroad station. On previous trips, French rail workers had helped by placing a sign, THIS EXIT FOR CAMPERS, on one exit door, and he had led the children through it with ease. He was not sure if the mayor of Annemasse, Jean Deffaugt, had alerted the workers that he was coming today.

"Where are you heading?" a soldier asked as Loinger was lining up the children.

"To the railroad reception center in town."

Don't worry, the soldier assured him. He would expedite the matter. He could see how tired the children were. He would just explain to the police that the children were with the soldiers. So fifty German soldiers, singing at the top of their lungs, led the children out of the station to the reception center, where Mayor Deffaugt was waiting with food.

Later that afternoon, Loinger tucked a soccer ball under his arm and took the children to a small field hidden in the woods. For the first three years of the German occupation in France, the Swiss had made it extremely difficult for refugees to enter their country. Surrounded by Germany and German-occupied countries, the Swiss did not want to give the Germans any justification to invade their country. Passports, French exit visas, and documents from German authorities were required to enter Switzerland. Border guards often turned back adults.

But recently, the Swiss had agreed not to deport children under sixteen, even if they came into the country illegally. With the recent Soviet army victory over the German army at Stalingrad and the massive Soviet offense launched against the Germans, the outcome of the war now seemed uncertain. Switzerland had adjusted its policies, both to protect itself and for humanitarian reasons.

The field was less than a mile from the barbed-wire fence separating France from Switzerland. Loinger organized the children for the most important game of their lives. There were no uniforms. No one wore cleats or shin guards. He marked off the playing field. Two teams of eleven players each were formed. He reviewed the rules for those who had never played soccer before. The younger children were seated on the sidelines, but he promised they would get a chance to play, too.

He walked onto the field, took his place as referee, and blew the whistle for the first soccer game to begin. Before long the children were playing seriously, intent on their team winning.

As prearranged, when night fell, a member of the Maquis, the French resistance movement, came to tell Loinger that it was safe now for the children to cross into Switzerland. Loinger led the children to the barbed-wire fence. He explained that on the other side of that fence a man would be waiting for them, and they should not be frightened when they saw that he was wearing a uniform. This man would escort them to a place where they would be safe. Living arrangements would then be found for them until the war was over. Once he felt certain that the children understood what he was saying, he stretched the barbed-wire fence and watched them slip through it and cross to safety.

Between twelve and fifteen thousand Jewish children were smuggled into Switzerland or Spain — neutral countries during the war — or lived out the war in France with sympathetic Christian families or in convents and church schools. In late 1944, Georges Loinger, his wife, and their two-year-old son also slipped through the wire fence into Switzerland.

"You Do Not Know the Extent of My Courage"

ANNEMASSE, OCCUPIED FRANCE

Marianne Cohn

By May 1944, the Maquis, the French national resistance movement, had stepped up its guerrilla warfare against the Germans, and many French people believed that they would soon have their country back. But Jews were still being deported to concentration camps. The Jewish Scouts and the Zionist Youth Movement continued smuggling children over the border into Switzerland. In April, when the Nazis captured scout Mila Racine, twenty-two-year-old Marianne Cohn took Racine's place. On May 31, 1944, the Nazis caught Cohn and twenty-eight children on their way to the Swiss border. They were hauled off to jail in Annemasse.

Screams of people being tortured pierced the long hours until dawn. Locked alone in her cell, Cohn could not comfort the children. She knew how frightened and lost they must feel. Seventeen of them were under fourteen. One was only three.

Marianne knew about fear, and displacement, and loss. She had no idea where her parents and sister were now. Still, Marianne had been luckier than many Jewish teenagers. When she was seventeen, she was sent to a Jewish Scout camp on a farm in the unoccupied zone of France. There she found community and a reason to live by helping others. She knew the children would be even more frightened tomorrow, when the Gestapo interrogated them. She knew what it would be like for them: one Gestapo officer seated at a desk with his revolver pointed at them; another Nazi seated in front of a typewriter, his whip resting on the desk. Question after question: What's your name? Your address? Who brought you here? Where did you get these documents? And always, the hammering punctuation after each question. Are you Jewish?

She felt some relief two days later upon learning that Annemasse's mayor, Jean Deffaugt, who had forged many documents for Jews and helped many escape to Switzerland, had convinced the Nazi commandant to send the seventeen youngest children to a local orphanage.

Every morning for three days, Cohn and the remaining eleven children were paraded from jail through town to Nazi headquarters in the Hôtel de France to work in the kitchen. At night she was interrogated and beaten. The Maquis got word to her that they could arrange her escape. She declined, knowing that the commandant would murder all the children if she escaped. Her duty was to stay with the children to the very end. She refused to abandon them. Near

Marianne Cohn

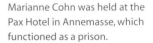

Marianne Cohn was held at the Pax Hotel in Annemasse, which functioned as a prison.

death in her cell, Marianne Cohn mustered the only power she had to protect the children and wrote a poem:

Interior of the Pax Hotel–turned prison

I will betray tomorrow, not today.
Today, tear off my fingernails.
I will not betray!
You do not know the extent of my courage.
I know.
You are five hands, harsh and full of rings.
You are wearing hob-nailed boots.

I will betray tomorrow. Not today.
Tomorrow.
I need the night to make up my mind.
I need at least one night
to disown, to abjure, to betray.
To disown my friends,
To abjure bread and wine,
To betray life,
to die.

I will betray tomorrow, not today.
The file is under the windowpane.
The file is not meant for the torturer.
The file is not meant for the executioner.
The file is for my wrists.

Today, I do not have anything to say.
I will betray tomorrow.

On the night of July 8, Marianne and three other imprisoned members of the Maquis were dragged out and murdered. Two weeks later, the Nazi commandant informed Deffaugt that all the children "had to disappear." Deffaugt got word to Maquis fighters in the area, who gave him the following message for the SS officer: *The German occupation is coming to an end. If you kill the children, you'll pay with your life, as we have your address in Germany. But if you don't touch them, we will let you escape to Switzerland.*

Plaque honoring Marianne Cohn, Annemasse

On August 18, the Germans in Annemasse surrendered to the Maquis. That same day, the children were taken over the border to Switzerland, just in case the Maquis lost control of the area.

Children who survived the war thanks to Marianne Cohn, Mila Racine, and Jean Deffaugt, August 18, 1944

IN THE FORESTS

The dense forests and swamps of Eastern Europe offered cover for Jews fleeing the Nazis. But unlike Jews in France, Belgium, Holland, and Greece, who often found aid and sympathy among the populace, eastern European Jews found themselves almost exclusively in enemy territory in their own countries. Entrenched anti-Semitism among the local population and the Nazi threat of death to anyone who helped Jews produced few allies. Jewish councils in many ghettos urged the young not to escape, reminding them that the Germans would retaliate against those left behind, and this was no idle threat. The Jewish Council in Minsk, Belorussia (now Belarus), was among the few councils that actively encouraged Jews to escape the ghetto, and more than ten thousand escaped with the council's help.

Tens of thousands of Jews fled the ghettos and wandered about the woods with no permanent shelter or food. A lucky few were taken in by Soviet partisans or by established Jewish family camps. Historians believe there were as many as 22,400 Jewish partisans and 13,500 Jews living in family camps in the forests. But most Jews who fled to the forest eventually starved to death or were murdered by their anti-Semitic countrymen.

Partisans from the Leninski-Komsomol unit, Nacza, Belorussia

Jewish partisans,
Markuszów, Poland, 1943

Among those who fled into the forests were four brothers from the small village of Stankevich, in western Belorussia (now Belarus): Tuvia, Asael, Zus, and Archik Bielski. Tuvia, the eldest brother, was determined to save as many Jews as possible, regardless of their age or health. The Bielskis formed a self-sufficient village in the middle of a forest surrounded by the enemy. The camp evolved into a "shtetl," like many of the small, provincial towns with large Jewish populations in eastern Europe that existed and flourished before the Holocaust.

Background image:
Forest in Lower Silesia, near
Sobótka, Poland

49

A Shtetl in the Wilderness

NALIBOKI FOREST, OCCUPIED BELORUSSIA

The Bielski family before the war, Stankevich, Poland, ca. 1925–1935

Tuvia Bielski

With the arrival of the Germans in Belorussia, the Bielski family shared the fate of thousands of other Jews. Their parents, two brothers, and Zus's wife and child were murdered in one of many mass killings. For a short while, thirty-five-year-old Tuvia, thirty-three-year-old Asael, and twenty-nine-year-old Zus found refuge in barns and in the homes of Christian friends. But when a friend was tortured and died, refusing to reveal their whereabouts, the three brothers moved into the forest. The Germans tracked down the youngest brother, twelve-year-old Archik, and ordered him to lead them to his brothers. Archik refused and was made to dig his own grave. For some still-unknown reason, the Nazis let Archik go. Shortly after, he joined his brothers in the forest, bringing ten relatives.

Asael and Zus relished the idea of raiding German food supplies, destroying communications systems, and blowing up

50

bridges, rail tracks, and trains in retaliation. Tuvia wanted revenge, too, but insisted that saving Jews was more important: "I would rather save one old Jewish woman than kill ten Nazi soldiers." He sent guides back to the labor camps and ghettos with a clear and direct message: everyone was welcome to join them in the forest. The more of them there were, he argued, the better each person's chance to survive.

Asael Bielski

Despite massacres of more than eighteen thousand Jews in the area, it was not easy convincing people to seek refuge in the forest. Surviving there required ingenuity, courage, stamina, and luck. The Bielskis were used to living without comforts. They had grown up in a two-room wooden hut with a straw roof and clay floors and no running water or electricity. Everyone in the encampment had to work unless they were ill. Shelters of wood and straw had to be built. Water and food had to be gathered.

Gradually more and more people sought out the Bielski family camp. To maintain order and discipline, the brothers organized it like the military. People were expected to follow orders without question. Tuvia, a natural leader and the eldest brother, was voted camp commander. Asael was second in command. Zus was in charge of intelligence gathering. Archik's knowledge of the woods made him a natural courier.

On August 1, 1943, Asael had just returned from a triumphant three-week food- and supply-gathering expedition when the Germans launched a massive military operation: fifty-two thousand soldiers, along with *Einsatzgruppen* (mobile killing units of German SS and police, and local collaborators) against the partisans living

Zusya (Zus) Bielski

in the nearby forests. Sounds of planes flying overhead and German guns firing were heard at the camp. People began running about and screaming. Tuvia knew there was no practical way to fight the Germans: they were too powerful and too many. The forest's thick canopy of leaves was inadequate armor for the seven hundred people in their camp. He assumed that the Germans had already blocked all the exits from the forest.

He had to stay calm and act fast before the situation became totally chaotic. He galloped into the center of camp, raised his rifle, and ordered everyone to stop and form rows like soldiers. His voiced was pained as he shouted, "Jews! Have mercy! Don't lose your minds. If we don't keep together and stay calm, we will all be lost. We have hope that we will get out of this. You must listen only to me." His commanding, confident manner quieted them, but the truth was that he had no plan.

Michal Mechlis and Akiva Szymonowicz offered a possible solution. A forest surveyor, Mechlis knew the woods well. So did Szymonowicz, a peddler. They told Tuvia that seven miles away, deep in the swamp, was a tiny island called Krasnaya Gorka ("Beautiful Hill"). Mechlis doubted the Germans even knew about it. Perhaps they could evade the enemy by hiding there.

Tuvia explained the strenuous journey ahead to everyone. Much of it would be through swamp. They would travel only at night, when their movements could not be as easily tracked. They would march in single file to leave the fewest footprints. They would carry very little, and absolutely nothing could be discarded along the way, since even the smallest item could lead the enemy to them.

Hundreds of people lined up in the hot, humid night air to begin the journey. Parents carrying small children were put at the head of the line. Men with weapons took up the rear. As they moved from the woods into the swamp, the mud thickened and deepened. People's feet sank into the dark slime, and they could barely lift one leg in front of the other. In some places the mud was up to their chests, sometimes up to their necks. Men with weapons held them over their heads to keep them dry. People grabbed trees and bushes for support. One young man tied himself to his mother, fearful of losing her in the muck. They slogged on for three hours, finally reaching shallow water but having covered only two miles.

At midnight a loudspeaker in the distance boomed in Russian, then in Polish: "Partisans, you know you cannot fight a war against our tanks and cannons. When daylight comes, throw down your guns and surrender."

Still they pressed on, sweaty, grimy, and hungry.

At dawn they found a dry spot and stopped. They ate some of the grains of wheat and rye, dried peas, and turnips stuffed in their pockets, even though the food was now covered with mud. They tried to sleep. Anyone who snored was awakened lest the sound carry. Tuvia set out with two men to see if the Germans might have abandoned the search.

As they neared their former camp, they heard twigs crack but didn't see anything. Then they heard machine-gun fire and someone shouting in German, "Catch the Jews!" They retreated on their hands and knees back through the bushes.

When they returned to the group, panic had set in again: everyone had heard the machine guns. Tuvia rallied the group to move on. As before, all walked in silence. Tall, sharp grasses scraped their arms and faces. But the thick vegetation was also a blessing because it provided some cover from the bombers flying overhead. The grasses gave way to more mud. Again they tied themselves to one another with belts and ropes, fearful of drowning.

After eight days, they reached a flooded area with good tree cover. Tuvia tied the strap of his submachine gun to his belt, wound it around himself and a tree so he wouldn't slip into the water, and dozed off. Some people searched for food but found only a few raspberry bushes. The next morning was sunny, but everyone was too exhausted and hungry to appreciate it. They got ready to march on with no idea of how much farther they had to go. Almost immediately they came to Krasnaya Gorka! The island was too small for all seven hundred to sit on. Some people plopped themselves down in the muddy water around it. Tuvia took a head count. Six people were missing, including two children. He sent scouts to find them. They returned with all six that evening.

While on the island, two men standing guard heard rustling in the bushes. A wet, ragged woman appeared. She claimed that she'd lost her way from her village. The guards didn't believe her; the marsh was off any route to any village. Tuvia questioned her intensely. Finally, after being hit several times, she confessed that she was spying for the Germans. Letting her go was not an option. Among partisans there was no mercy for collaborators. Tuvia ordered her shot.

For two more days, the seven hundred people sat silently in unbearable heat, wet and desperately hungry. Constant machine-gun fire, the barking of attack dogs, and the shouting of German soldiers echoed all around them. They had no food left. They drank water from the muddy swamp. They found the carcass of a dead horse and ate its rotting meat. Tuvia sent scouts to the nearest village to see if they might find food.

They returned empty-handed. The Germans were everywhere.

By the tenth day, blisters appeared around people's mouths. Stomachs swelled. Tuvia knew that if people did not eat soon, they would die. Zus and eight men set out for the Bielskis' native village of Stankevich, hoping their former neighbors would give them food.

Two more days passed, and Zus and his men did not return. Tuvia felt there was no choice other than to go back toward the villages to find food. He put his most experienced men in charge of groups of twenty or thirty and staggered their departures. Tuvia and Asael brought up the rear with the weakest. As before, they struggled through the terrain. Along the trail they saw crumpled German cigarette packs, used cartridges, and newspapers. Was this a sign that the Germans were gone?

Partisan dugout, Naliboki forest, Belorussia (now Belarus)

At the Niemen River at the edge of the forest, they found a small boat. Some people swam across. One person drowned. The scattered units regrouped. Scouts searching for food learned from friendly peasants that the Germans had burned 150 villages in the area and killed almost five thousand locals. Twenty-one thousand non-Jews, including four thousand children, had been sent to forced-labor camps.

But *they* had survived. It seemed like a miracle. Seven hundred starving, weakened people had outwitted the mighty German army for two weeks.

Tuvia knew that now more Jews would flee to the forest. They could not survive on their own. He had to get ready for them. It was time to build a new camp.

For the next several months, the Bielski Jews traipsed from burned-out village to burned-out village, gathering food that had not been harvested or scorched. They dug up two hundred tons of potatoes and five tons of beets, cut down three tons of cabbages and five tons of wheat. Other crews lugged back windows, heaters, boilers, stoves, and barrels. Foundations were dug for permanent structures. The floors were tree trunks tied together with barbed wire and covered with moss. Branches covered with earth camouflaged the roofs so German pilots would not see the shelters. Most structures had room for forty people sleeping on straw-covered wooden benches along the walls. The only light was from a tiny window and the open door.

The camp was organized like a town: a main street with huts on either side. People lined up for soup and bread cooked in the communal kitchen. Children got a daily portion of milk. Any milk left over was given to the women and the elderly. There were ritual slaughterhouses, where the chickens and cows were killed according to Jewish dietary laws. Three barbers gave haircuts and shaves.

There were factories for sausage making and watches, a tannery, a bakery, a flour mill, and carpentry, shoemaking, and saddler shops. Carpenters made stocks for the rifles and submachine guns, plus windows and door frames. They made the barrels for the tanners to soak and cure the animal skins used by the shoemakers and saddlers. A prized possession in the camp was the light-yellow leather boots they made. The blacksmiths shod the horses and made charcoal from burned trees. Metalworkers repaired old weapons and made new ones. Partisans in other forest camps brought their weapons here to be cleaned and repaired. Hundreds of people working together — talking, gossiping, and joking — made them forget their personal tragedies for a while.

The younger boys tended the horses. The older boys guarded the cows and helped in the kitchens. Some became apprentices in the workshops. In summer the younger children collected berries. There was never enough dark brown soap made from discarded cow's milk and ashes to battle lice. Patients lined up to see the doctor and his wife, a nurse. The doctor visited the huts of those too weak to come to him. A hospital was built a mile away for people with contagious diseases. Friendly locals in nearby towns ordered and delivered

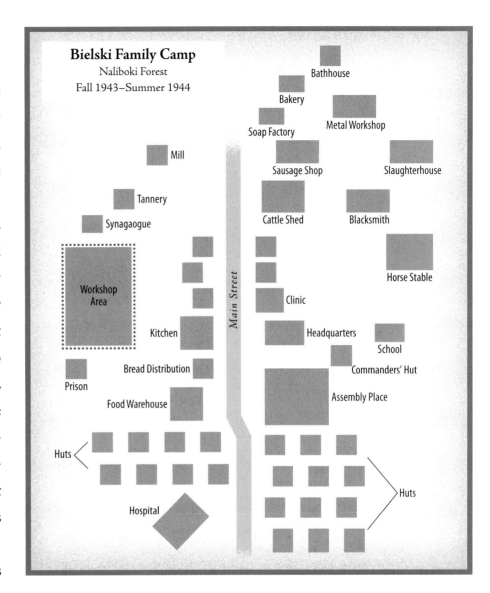

Bielski Family Camp
Naliboki Forest
Fall 1943–Summer 1944

Bathhouse
Bakery
Metal Workshop
Soap Factory
Mill
Sausage Shop
Slaughterhouse
Tannery
Synagaogue
Cattle Shed
Blacksmith
Main Street
Horse Stable
Workshop Area
Clinic
Kitchen
Headquarters
School
Bread Distribution
Commanders' Hut
Prison
Assembly Place
Food Warehouse
Huts
Hospital
Huts

In the Bielski family camp,
Naliboki forest, May 1944

medicines, but there were never enough available. In spite of inadequate medicine, poor nutrition, and crowding, almost no one in the camp died. The camp evolved into a self-sufficient village of 1,230 Jews, a "shtetl" in the heart of the Naliboki wilderness.

In July 1944, the Soviet army won back control of the area near the Bielski encampment, and the Germans fled. The Soviets ordered the Bielski Jews to leave the forest. They packed up their few possessions, uncertain of what was ahead. In their former towns and cities, all traces of their lives and of Jewish life had been destroyed. Most of their loved ones had been murdered.

Former Bielski partisans celebrate in Israel, ca. 1949–1950
(Zus Bielski and his son Yakov at bottom left)

Asael died fighting in the Soviet army. Tuvia, Zus, and Archik (Aron) eventually settled in the United States. Today, the children, grandchildren, and great-grandchildren of the 1,230 Jews who survived in the Bielski camp number over twelve thousand.

PART THREE
IN THE GHETTOS

Broken people,

Walking along the street.

The transport is leaving for Poland.

Old ones go, and young ones go.

Healthy ones go, and sick ones go,

Not knowing if they will survive.

Transport "A" went.

And more went too.

Thousands died

And nothing helped.

The German weasel

Wants more and more blood.

— Zdeněk Weinberger, Theresienstadt ghetto, occupied Czechoslovakia,

age twelve, ca. 1942–1944

THE FINAL SOLUTION

The mass murder of Jews began in June 1941, soon after Germany broke its nonaggression pact with the Soviet Union and took over some of its territory.

A woman awaits execution, Lubny, the Ukraine

In one week in September 1941, mobile killing squads of German SS and police, working with local collaborators, shot 33,771 Jewish men, women, and children outside Kiev, in the Ukraine, and murdered tens of thousands more near Vilna (now called Vilnius), Lithuania. Over the next three years, mobile killing units gunned down approximately 1.3 million Jews, around 30,000 Roma and Sinti (Gypsies), as many as 200,000 officials of the Soviet Communist Party and the Soviet State, and millions of other Soviet civilians in the territory of the German-occupied Soviet Union.

On January 20, 1942, Nazi officials met in secret at a lakeside villa in Wannsee, Berlin. There they mapped out their plan for what they called the Final Solution of the Jewish Question: in anticipation of their domination of Europe, the Nazis aimed to exterminate an estimated eleven million Jews. This number included Jews even in countries not then under German control, such as Great Britain and the entire Soviet Union.

A Jew is executed by a German soldier at the edge of a mass grave, Vinnitsa, the Ukraine, January 1942

For a scheme of such grand proportions, mass shootings proved inefficient. Bullets were costly and murders on such a large scale could not be hidden from local populations. It was also psychologically difficult, and men broke down under the strain of killing men, women, and children day after day in village after village. Gassing vans replaced the mobile killing units, but they proved inefficient, too, so death camps were built. A highly organized system of transporting millions to these camps was planned.

In eastern Europe, where there were more Jews than anywhere else on the continent, the Nazis first rounded up Jews from rural areas and small villages and forced them to migrate to larger cities. Once in the cities, Jews were segregated from the non-Jewish populace: corralled into the poorest and least desirable sections of the cities and forbidden to leave without permission. The idea of separating Jews from the rest of the population was not new. The first "ghetto" was created in Venice in 1516.

Ghettos were collection points, temporary holding pens, and the last stop before deportation to labor and death camps. Between 1939 and 1945, the Nazis established twelve hundred ghettos in the countries they occupied.

In December 1941, couriers from the Jewish underground of

Reporters examine a van suspected of being used to gas Jews, Chelmno death camp, Poland, 1945

The wall dividing Warsaw into small and large ghettos

Vilna, Lithuania, came to the ghetto in Warsaw, the capital of Poland, with the news that five thousand Vilna Jews had been murdered. Killing units had marched them out of the city and executed them in pits in the nearby forest. An escapee from the Chelmno death camp described gassings there. Most elders in the Warsaw ghetto rejected the idea that the Germans were conducting mass murder; it was just too monstrous to believe. In the last war, the Germans had occupied Poland, and the Poles had largely experienced them as a civilized people.

Jewish Council members insisted that nothing like that could happen in Warsaw. It was the largest ghetto in Poland. How could the Germans possibly murder its more than 375,000 Jews? Many young people, on the other hand, believed the reports. They visited people in their homes and related what they had heard. Few believed them.

Seven months later, the Germans told Adam Czerniakow, the head of Warsaw's Jewish Council, to prepare the first of many lists of Jews to be deported. The Jewish police were ordered to round up six thousand people per day. In keeping with the Nazi policy of deception, the Jews would be told that they were being "transferred to the East" to be "resettled." Czerniakow was not deceived. He realized that he would be sending people to their deaths; he pleaded with Nazi officials to at least exclude children from the order. When they refused, he committed suicide rather than be a party to the genocide. He wrote to his wife: "They want me to kill the children, this I cannot do."

The Nazis promised other council members that their families would be spared if they drew up the deportation lists. Pink posters stating that three kilograms of bread and one kilogram of jam would be given to all who "voluntarily resettled" were plastered all over the ghetto. The offer of food lured thousands of starving Jews. Every night young people ripped the posters down and replaced them with their own posters, reading DEPORTATION IS TREBLINKA AND TREBLINKA IS DEATH. Every morning Jewish police put the pink posters back up. Jewish youths went door-to-door telling people that deportation would lead to certain death. Still, few Jews were ready to believe it.

On July 22, 1942, the Treblinka death camp was opened, and the roundups began. The Jewish police stormed through the ghetto, dragging people out of their homes and beating anyone who resisted. When the Jewish police did not meet their daily quota, the SS, German police, and other collaborators joined the hunt for victims. By the twenty-first of September, more than 300,000 Jews had been deported to Treblinka or murdered during the roundups.

The deportation of Warsaw's Jews

The Warsaw Ghetto Uprising

Mordechai Anielewicz

Twenty-three-year-old Mordechai Anielewicz was away from Warsaw during the deportations, traveling to other ghettos in Poland to warn Jews of the mass murders that had already taken place. When word of the roundups reached him, he raced back to Warsaw to find that the ghetto population had been reduced to a fraction of its former size. The seventy thousand remaining Jews were now divided into three areas, separated by abandoned buildings and deserted streets.

The Nazis' methodical system of mass roundups shocked Warsaw's older Jews, who had so far avoided deportation. They realized that they should have believed the young people. They should have hidden or fought back. Tens of thousands might still have died, but perhaps not three hundred thousand. Warsaw's Jews now vowed that they would not be taken without a fight.

Among those deported were thousands of Zionist youths. Anielewicz began the hard work of rebuilding his partisan forces, the Jewish Fighting Organization (ZOB). A separate underground resistance group, the Jewish Military Union (ŻZW), was also formed. Anielewicz first set out to eliminate Jewish collaborators. A Jewish guard in a German factory who had cruelly mistreated Jewish workers was beaten and had acid poured on his face. Thirteen Jewish police officers who had assisted in the roundups, including the top commander, were assassinated.

Jews who still had money were pressed to give it up so the ZOB

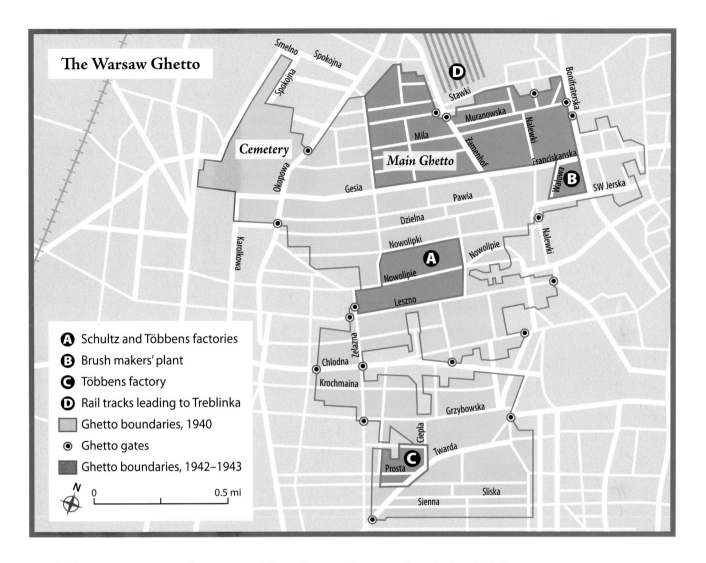

The Warsaw Ghetto

A Schultz and Többens factories
B Brush makers' plant
C Többens factory
D Rail tracks leading to Treblinka
Ghetto boundaries, 1940
⊙ Ghetto gates
Ghetto boundaries, 1942–1943

N 0   0.5 mi

Cemetery

Main Ghetto

could buy weapons. When a wealthy salt merchant refused, the ZOB kidnapped his son and released him only after he contributed. The ZOB stole money and valuables from anyone they could — smugglers, speculators, police officers, and factory owners. They raided the cashier's office of the Jewish Council.

Unfortunately the money did not bring many weapons. The Polish Home Army, one of the two main military organizations of the Polish underground, refused to share its large stock of arms. Poles were not being murdered like the Jews were; Nazi policy did not call for the extermination of the Polish people, so the Polish Home Army wanted to wait and stage their own uprising when their chances of success would be better. In the meantime, they didn't want to risk any of their ammunition on the ZOB action. Warsaw's Jews knew they had run out of time. They were forced to buy weapons from arms dealers in the Aryan section of Warsaw, who charged outrageous prices because they knew how desperately the Jews needed them.

Once acquired, the weapons had to be smuggled into the ghetto. Tunnels were dug from the ghetto to the Aryan side of Warsaw. One tunnel was barely more than three feet high by three feet wide. The resisters had to crawl on all fours, holding their weapons. Sometimes they threw the weapons over the wall. Couriers carrying guns entered the ghettos at the end of a day, along with other Jewish workers returning from labor sites.

Photo used in the false ID card for underground courier Feigele Peltel, 18 years old

Eighteen-year-old Feigele Peltel, with her red hair and perfect Polish, did not look Jewish and easily deceived the guards at the ghetto gate. She flirted with them and convinced them that she was only a Polish smuggler, hoping to sell butter to the suffering Jews. She bribed them, and they never searched her. They did not find the ten pounds of dynamite she had wrapped in greasy paper.

Twenty-eight-year-old Frumke Plotnicka looked just like all the other exhausted Jews returning to the ghetto after a day of work in German factories outside. Guards searched the sack of potatoes over her shoulder but didn't bother to reach all the way down to the bottom, where the pistols lay.

On the snow-covered morning of January 18, 1943, when the temperature was −4°F, armed vehicles roared into the ghetto, catching the ZOB off guard. Two hundred German soldiers and armed Lithuanian and Latvian military followed. Their orders were to round up eight thousand Jews who did not have legal working permits. The soldiers marched from building to building, shouting for people to come down to the street. To their great astonishment, few obeyed. Instead, people ran to their hiding places in attics, cupboards, and walls. Desperate to meet their eight-thousand-Jew quota, the troops picked up Jews with legal work permits, including members of the Jewish Council.

From his headquarters at 18 Mila Street, Mordechai Anielewicz watched the soldiers herd their captives toward the *Umschlagplatz*, the assembly point. He ordered his nine soldiers to hide their weapons under their clothing and sneak into the procession. At the *Umschlagplatz*, seventeen-year-old Margalit Landau threw the first grenade. And then, with only a few pistols and bullets among them, the nine attacked. Anielewicz and three other resisters survived the skirmish.

That afternoon German soldiers bounded up four flights of stairs at 58 Zamenhof Street, where ZOB's deputy commander, Yitzhak Zuckerman, and his unit of forty were stationed. Their arsenal consisted of only four pistols, four grenades, a few Molotov cocktails, and assorted knives and iron pipes. A German soldier burst into the ZOB apartment, expecting to find a band of guerrilla fighters, but he saw only Zacharia Artstein calmly reading a book. The soldier ran into the next room to see if there was anyone else around, and Artstein shot him in the back.

Yitzhak Zuckerman in Warsaw after the war, June 8, 1946

Hearing gunfire, the other soldiers in the building fled. Zuckerman's unit escaped over the rooftops with only one casualty.

Molotov cocktails and gunfire greeted German patrols as they marched down other streets. Sixty ZOB fighters were apprehended. When they refused to board the cattle cars, they were shot.

Violence mounted over the next three days as more than fourteen hundred armed troops invaded the ghetto. In spite of their numbers and their weapons, they managed to round up only sixty-five hundred Jews, mostly the sick and elderly. After four days, the Germans withdrew. No one knew when the next roundup might happen, but no one doubted that the Germans would be back.

A model cross section showing an example of a bunker and passageways

Anielewicz organized the remaining ZOB into twenty-two fighting units of ten to twelve people each. Nine units were set up in the central ghetto. Eight units were stationed in the German workshops in the Többens-Schultz area. Another five units were set up in the brush makers' district. The Jewish Military Union (ŹZW) had 250 fighters. Most partisans were between the ages of nineteen and twenty-five. These young men and women did not have the responsibility of caring for children or elderly parents and so were free to focus on the task that history had forced upon them. They lived, ate, and trained together.

Anielewicz harbored no illusion that the

ZOB would ultimately triumph, but he was determined to die fighting. Plans were made for the next German assault. With too few fighters, too few weapons, and no one with military experience or knowledge of warfare, they would have to rely on guerrilla tactics: hit-and-run actions, ambushing the enemy from roofs, balconies, and windows, then retreating unseen through back alleys and intricate underground passages. Most likely the Germans would not venture into the ghetto's maze of narrow streets, since that would be walking into a snare.

Holes were knocked into the attic walls of connected buildings so the fighters could move from one position to another without going out in the open. They laid ladders from rooftop to rooftop and practiced running across them until it was second nature. They practiced racing through a network of basement bunkers and alley passageways. They learned the mechanics of how a gun worked, how to take it apart and clean it. They practiced shooting at targets without bullets by looking through the gun sight, taking aim, then gently squeezing the trigger. They dug tunnels and planted explosives near German headquarters and sentry posts. Thirteen-year-old Lusiak Blones scoured the ghetto for material, looking in garbage cans, residences, and empty warehouses for metal pipes and bottles. When he couldn't find enough, he took lightbulbs. The ZOB created explosives by putting sulfuric acid inside the metal pipes, bottles, and lightbulbs. They carved slits into the pipes, so that when the pipes exploded, metal scattered everywhere. Jewish laborers making German uniforms in factories outside the ghetto smuggled in pants and jackets so the fighters could disguise themselves as German soldiers if they needed to. Constant readiness was key: no one could leave a post without permission.

The Polish Home Army, impressed by the January action, finally gave the ZOB forty-nine pistols, fifty grenades, and nine pounds of explosives. But only thirty-six pistols worked. Anielewicz's request for more weapons was refused. But one sympathetic member of the Polish Home Army sneaked into the ghetto and helped set up a makeshift factory that produced more than two thousand grenades. Jews who had not given money before gave now. Anielewicz sent blue-eyed, blond-haired Zuckerman, who easily passed for a Christian, out to the Christian part of Warsaw to buy more weapons.

Warsaw's Jews moved underground. More than 631 fortified hiding places, called bunkers, were dug. The bunkers were hidden behind

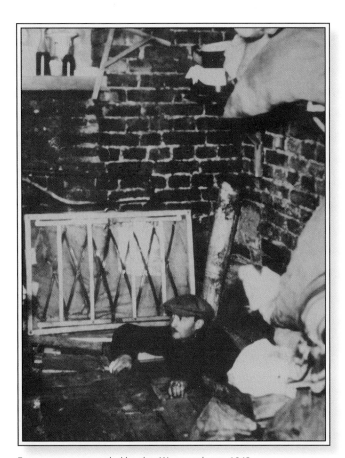
Entrance to a concealed bunker, Warsaw ghetto, 1943

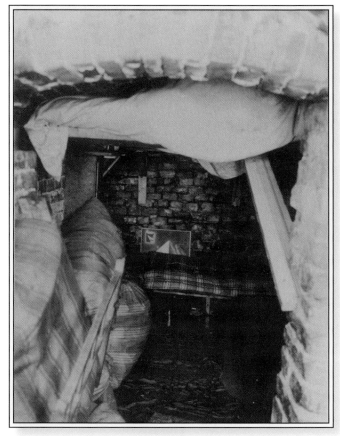
A bunker in the Warsaw ghetto

stoves, under toilets, between walls, under basements, and in attics. The larger, well-equipped ones had heat, electricity, a water supply, enough food to last for months, and sometimes a telephone. People built passageways connecting bunkers in adjoining buildings. They stacked furniture over their bunker entrances and piled sandbags over basement windows.

On April 18, 1943, Warsaw's Jews prepared for the first night of Passover, marking the journey of the ancient Hebrews from Egyptian slavery to freedom. Jews returning from work outside the ghetto reported that large numbers of armed Latvians were stationed every seventy-five feet along the outside ghetto wall. Anielewicz alerted his 750 fighters to get to their posts. Anielewicz did not know that the Germans had nearly 2,100 armed troops poised to attack. April 20 was Hitler's birthday. The Nazis wanted to give him the gift of a *Judenfrei* Warsaw—a Warsaw free of Jews—by that date.

At two a.m., a truck roared into the ghetto, bringing dozens of armed Latvians. Anielewicz notified all fighting units to hold their fire. Four hours later, hundreds of German soldiers, singing marching songs, advanced confidently into Nalewki Street. Behind them came light tanks, cannons, flamethrowers, and three vehicles with submachine guns.

A ZOB resister hurled the first grenade. Then another grenade was thrown, and another. For two hours, a steady flow of grenades, Molotov cocktails, and bullets rained down on the Germans, who hadn't expected an armed assault. When the SS officer in charge finally ordered his stunned troops to retreat, the street was strewn with German dead and wounded. Not one Jewish fighter had been injured. In the pause that followed, ZOB resisters rushed down to the streets to commandeer the helmets, weapons, and uniforms of their enemy's dead.

At the same time as this attack, grenades and Molotov cocktails greeted the German and Ukrainian units marching into Zamenhof Street. Hit from all sides, the startled soldiers scattered and fled toward buildings, seeking shelter, but all doorways were blocked. After a half hour, the foot soldiers withdrew and two light tanks rolled into the street. ZOB grenades blew up both tanks and their crews inside. When German ambulances sped in to pick up their wounded, the ZOB showed no mercy and threw grenades at the ambulances, too.

The battle resumed on Nalewki Street. The Germans stacked mattresses as barricades. ZOB Molotov cocktails set the mattresses on fire as ZOB fighters on roofs and at windows let go with a hail of bullets.

German soldiers shell a housing block during the Warsaw Ghetto Uprising, 1943

The Germans retreated again but managed first to torch a building where ZOB fighters were positioned.

SS general Jürgen Stroop ordered cannon fire on the buildings at the intersection of Zamenhof and Mila Streets. But the cannons' roar brought no response; the ZOB troops were already gone. Tanks provided cover fire as small German assault units advanced. Smoke engulfed many buildings, forcing the ZOB to flee.

That evening the battle moved to Muranowska Street. With one light machine gun, the ZOB held back the Germans and retrieved two machine guns and a number of rifles. Stroop withdrew his forces and ordered security tightened along the wall and at all twenty-two ghetto gates. He stationed soldiers on the rooftops of buildings abutting the ghetto on the Aryan side of Warsaw and ordered them to fire into the ghetto all night.

On the third day of the uprising, amid the endless bursts of gunfire and explosions, two resisters climbed to the roof of the house at 17 Muranowska and fastened a hand-sewn blue-and-white flag to a chimney. Blue and white are the colors of the *tallit*, or prayer shawl, and were the colors of the Zionist movement's flag.

At midnight, the ZOB received a message from the Polish Home Army demanding that the Polish flag be raised. The Jews replied that they did not have one, so the Home Army threw the red-and-white Polish flag into the sewer with a note of where it should be delivered. The resisters collected it from the sewer. Two more men climbed up to the roof. By dawn, the two flags flew side by side. The Germans tried to shoot down the flags but failed.

That night Mordechai Anielewicz wrote to Yitzhak Zuckerman, who was still in the Aryan part of Warsaw, trying to buy more weapons.

What happened exceeded our boldest dreams. The Germans ran twice from the ghetto. One of our companies held out for forty minutes, and another for more than six hours. The mine set in the "brush makers" area exploded. Several of our companies attacked the dispersing Germans. Our losses in manpower are minimal. This is also an achievement. . . . I feel that great things are happening and what we dared to do is of great, enormous importance. . . .

Beginning from today we shall shift over to the partisan tactic. Three battle companies will move out tonight, with two tasks: reconnaissance and obtaining arms. . . . Short-range weapons are of no use to us. . . . What we need urgently: grenades, rifles, machine guns, and explosives.

It is impossible to describe the conditions under which the Jews of the ghetto are now living. Only a few will be able to hold out. The remainder will die sooner or later. Their fate is decided. In almost all the hiding places in which thousands are concealing themselves it is not possible to light a candle for lack of air. With the aid of our transmitter we heard the marvelous report on our fight by the "Shavit" radio station. The fact that we are remembered beyond the ghetto walls encourages us in our struggle.

Peace go with you, my friend! Perhaps we may still meet again! The dream of my life has risen to become fact. . . . Self-defense in the ghetto will have been a reality. Jewish armed resistance and revenge are facts. I have been a witness to the magnificent, heroic fighting of Jewish men in battle.

Stroop decided that the only way to force the Jews out of their hiding places was to set the entire ghetto on fire. He spent the night planning to burn Warsaw's Jews alive. As the days passed and as German troops attacked, flamethrowers torched buildings street by street, apartment house by apartment house. The fires destroyed much of the

Warsaw burning, 1943

food and water in the bunkers. Electricity failed, and whatever food was left could not be cooked. Children were fed first. Anger and fear built as people lived in complete silence so they would not alert the enemy overhead to their presence. Surrounded by smoke and fire, the resisters could not see to shoot at their enemies. They were constantly on the move through their network of attached attics, trying to stay ahead of the flames.

Marek Edelman

ZOB commander Marek Edelman looked out at the burning, collapsing buildings around him. If his unit was to survive, it had to move to the central ghetto. He ordered his fighters to wrap rags around their shoes to muffle their footsteps. Hot stones and melting glass from shattered windows seared the bottoms of their feet as they walked through suffocating smoke. Reaching a gap in a wall, they were blinded by a searchlight. A fighter shot out the light, and they all jumped through the opening.

Day after day, the Germans set more buildings afire. Smoke, gas, and flames flushed thousands of Jews out of their bunkers into the open air, at which point they were captured or shot. Many more jumped to their deaths trying to escape. Those who didn't evacuate their bunkers were either burned alive or suffocated. Entire streets where buildings had once stood were reduced to mere rows of charred frames. The stench of burned bodies was everywhere.

Jews are flushed from their bunkers, April 1943

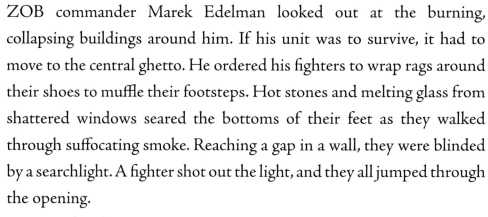

By April 24, the Germans had captured more than twenty thousand of Warsaw's remaining Jews. Thousands more had been shot or died in their bunkers. Stroop was convinced that the uprising would end soon. But the ZOB had no intention of surrendering.

On April 29, forty fighters under Eliezer Geller's command crept through the sewers, hoping to join partisan units and continue the fight against the Germans from outside the ghetto. When Stroop discovered that the Jews had been escaping through the sewers, he had dams built, which raised the water level of the sewers, drowning anyone who tried to use them. In answer, the Jews blew up the dams. So Stroop ordered his men to throw explosive charges, hand grenades, and smoke candles, which emitted toxic gases, into the sewers.

Bomber planes continued exploding buildings in the ghetto, and fires raged day and night, bringing unbearable heat. When sound detectors and bloodhounds discovered underground bunkers, gas was pumped into them. When the Jews emerged, gasping for air, they were shot. At night ZOB troops walked among the ruins, searching for survivors. More often they found the bodies of their dead comrades.

Anielewicz wrote to Zuckerman again on April 26:

A woman caught during the Warsaw Ghetto Uprising is guarded by SS, 1943

The number of men, women and children who fell victim to shooting and burning is immense. Our days are numbered, but as long as we have bullets we shall continue to defend ourselves. . . . As the end draws near, we demand of you: Remember how we were betrayed, the day will come when the spilling of our pure blood will be avenged.

A Jewish informer told Stroop the location of Anielewicz's head-quarters. On May 8, poison gas was pumped into 18 Mila Street.

Jews captured during the
Warsaw Ghetto Uprising, 1943

Rather than surrender, Anielewicz and more than one hundred fighters committed suicide. Marek Edelman and twenty-three other fighters in another bunker managed to escape the ghetto through the sewers.

In his report, General Stroop stated that 56,065 Jews were captured and sent to various camps, where most were murdered. More than seven thousand Jews were killed during the uprising. Another 6,929 were sent directly to Treblinka. Five or six thousand died in explosions or perished in fires. On May 16, 1943, Stroop blew up Warsaw's famed Tlomackie Street synagogue and cabled his superiors: "The Jewish quarter of Warsaw is no longer." He was mistaken. Some civilians and fighters hid successfully for months.

Background image:
Ruins of the Warsaw ghetto

Mass Actions in Ghettos and Camps in Eastern Occupied Europe

Sweden

Baltic Sea

Latvia

Soviet Union

Lithuania

Danzig

East Prussia

Greater Germany

Vilna
September 23, 1943

Minsk
August 1942–
October 21, 1943

Novogrudok
September 26, 1943

Mir
August 9, 1942

Nieswiesz
July 21, 1942

Treblinka
August 2, 1943

Bialystok
August 16, 1943

Koldichevo
March 17, 1944

Warsaw
April 19, 1943

Chelmno
January 17, 1945

Minsk Mazowiecki
January 10, 1943

Lakhva
September 3, 1942

Krushin
December 17, 1942

Sobibor
October 14, 1943

Lutsk
December 12, 1942

Czestochowa
January 4, 1943

Poland

Tuchin
September 24, 1942

Bedzin
August 3, 1943

Bohemia-Moravia

Brody
May 21–22, 1943

Kremenets
August 10, 1942

Soviet Union

Auschwitz-Birkenau
October 7, 1944

Lvov
November 19, 1943

Slovak Republic

Legend

✡ Uprising

🦅 Escape

⊕ Labor Camp

⊗ Death Camp

◉ Ghetto

∙∙∙ Nazi Germany/
Soviet Union
Partition

N

0 ___ 50 mi

0 ___ 50 km

Hungary

Romania

Poland illustrated with borders as they originally existed on September 28, 1939, the eve of German and Soviet invasions

Fifteen months later, on August 1, 1944, twenty-two members of the ZOB joined other Polish citizens in the Great Polish Uprising against the Germans, which failed. The Jewish fighters went back into hiding until the end of the war.

Marek Edelman survived the war and remained in Poland. Yitzhak Zuckerman and his wife, Zivia Lubetkin, along with Havka Folman and other resisters, founded the Ghetto Fighters' Kibbutz in Israel, which today includes a museum and a major research and educational center.

Zivia Lubetkin, ca. 1945–1949

"Scream the Truth at the World!"

THE RINGELBLUM ARCHIVE, WARSAW GHETTO, OCCUPIED POLAND

Emmanuel Ringelblum, imprisoned in the Warsaw ghetto, was a prominent historian. History and the written word are paramount to the Jewish people. Ringelblum kept a daily journal of the deterioration and desperation of ghetto life and the valiant effort by Jews to care for their people. In it he described how Jewish organizations banded together to feed thousands in soup kitchens. Food rations for Jews had been reduced to 184 calories a day. Most adults require a minimum of 2,000 calories a day. Malnutrition, overcrowding, and poor sanitation bred disease, and hundreds died every day. Weakening people physically and destroying their dignity were all part of the Nazi preparation for deporting Jews to the death camps.

Emmanuel Ringelblum

He described children dying in the streets and wrote about children, some as young as six, who risked their lives smuggling food into the ghetto for their families. Poet Henryka Lazowertówna immortalized these youngsters in a poem that was turned into a song and recited or sung at secret entertainments in the ghetto.

Starving children in the Warsaw ghetto

Over the walls, through holes, through the guard posts,
Through the wire, through the rubble, through the fence,
Hungry, cheeky, stubborn,
I slip through, I nip through like a cat.
At midday, in the night, at dawn,
In snowstorms, foul weather, and heat,
A hundred times I risk my life,
I stick out my childish neck.
A rough sack under my arm,
Wearing torn rags on my back,
With nimble young legs
And in my heart constant fear.
But you have to bear it all,
And you have to put up with it all,
So that tomorrow you
Will have your fill of bread.

Over the walls, through holes, through bricks,
At night, at dawn, and in day,
Cheeky, hungry, crafty,
I move as quietly as a shadow.
And if the hand of fate unexpectedly
Catches up with me one day in this game,
It is an ordinary trap of life.

Young smugglers breach the ghetto wall

Ringelblum wrote about how Jews defied the ban on cultural life. Famous singers performed in the streets to adoring crowds. Schools, theatrical groups, orchestras, writing clubs, discussion groups, and libraries were created to provide temporary solace and mental nourishment.

But Ringelblum knew that one person alone could not document the tragedy unfolding in Warsaw and all of Poland: "The whole truth, no matter how bitter, had to

Dotlinger, a famous opera singer, performs on the street, Warsaw ghetto, ca. 1941

be told." He might not survive this nightmare, but the truth had to. Every single fact had to be recorded so that when the war ended, "the world would read and know what the murderers had done." Then, perhaps, such brutality would never again happen to any people.

On November 22, 1940, one week after the ghetto was closed off, Ringelblum formed a secret group called *Oyneg Shabes* (or *Oneg Shabbat*), meaning "Joy of the Sabbath" in Hebrew, since its members usually met on Saturdays. He instructed his sixty "underground soldiers"—writers, scholars, rabbis, philosophers, poets, journalists, artists, and scientists—to collect as much as they could.

Underground newspapers countered Nazi lies and deception about the progress of the war, the death camps, and partisan successes. Young and old, professionals and nonprofessionals, described their struggles in letters, diaries, poems, and art. Tailors forced to make German military uniforms wrote about how they sabotaged production, sewing pant legs together incorrectly, reversing jacket sleeves, and putting buttons on backward and pockets on upside down. Partisans detailed how to make explosives. Szlamek Fajner, an escapee from the Chelmno death camp, where Jews were first gassed, described the mobile killing vans.

Rabbi Shimon Huberband wrote about Jews secretly observing their rituals, and collected all sorts of Yiddish jokes.

Rabbi Shimon Huberband

A teacher asks his pupil, "Tell me, Moyshe, what would you like to be if you were Hitler's son?" "An orphan," the pupil answers.

A Jew had all his worldly possessions taken from him, but he remained jolly and in good spirits. So his neighbor asked him: "All your possessions were taken away. Why are you still in good spirits?" The Jew answered: "My dear neighbor, they took away Czechoslovakia, Poland, Denmark, Belgium, Holland, France, and other countries. Someday, they will have to return all these countries. So then they'll have to return my things, too."

Janusz Korczak with children and staff members from his orphanage, Warsaw ghetto

By 1942, the archives contained more than thirty thousand items — theatrical posters, food-ration cards, photographs, underground newspapers, essays, drawings, and diaries.

The mass deportations began in July 1942. A witness had told Ringelblum about how Janusz Korczak, educator and director of an orphanage in Warsaw, led his two hundred children on their three-mile forced march to the cattle cars, as if in wordless protest against murder. Ringelblum knew that he could be taken any day. The Germans had not yet found out about the archive, but if they discovered it, they would certainly destroy it. He had to save this important work. On August 3, 1942, teacher Izrael Lichtensztajn and teenagers David Graber and Nachum Grzybacz buried ten metal boxes and three milk cans full of documents.

Nineteen-year-old Graber stuffed his own will into one can. In his final words, he expressed his pride in the archive and hope that it would be discovered after the war:

At the time I am writing this, no one may show the tip of his nose in the street. Neither is there security in the house. This is the fourteenth day of the gruesome process. Nearly all contact with our comrades has been lost. Each one on his own, each one tries to save one's life as best he can. The three of us are left. . . . We decided to write last wills. . . . We must hurry, we know not our time. We are at it till late in the night. . . .

It was clear to us we were creating a piece of history and that was more important than individual life. . . . Only [we] knew the place of burial. We would not divulge even if they cut pieces off us. I may with confidence say, this was the foundation and the propelling power in our existence. . . . Our work suffered not a moment's break. In the most difficult times we worked even more intensely. What we were unable to cry and shriek out to the world we buried in the ground. No thanks for me. It's not for thanks that I give my life and my strength.

I would love to see the moment in which the great treasure will be dug up and shriek to the world proclaiming the truth. So the world may know all. So the ones who did not live through it may be glad, and we may feel like veterans

Background image: Some of the boxes and one of the milk cans in which the Ringelblum Archives were buried *with medals on our chest. We would be the fathers, the teachers and educators of the future. We would be the grandfathers of the bards who tell to the grandsons, to the young the stories of victories and defeats, of keeping alive and of perishing. . . . But no, we shall certainly never live to see it, and therefore I do write my last will. May the treasure fall in good hands, may it last into better times, may it alarm and alert the world to what happened and was played out in the twentieth century. . . . We may die now in peace. We fulfilled our mission.*

Unearthing the archives in the former Warsaw ghetto, Poland, 1946

The only three survivors of the *Oyneg Shabes* group were present on September 18, 1946, when ten metal boxes and a milk can were dug up at 68 Nowolipki Street. On December 1, 1950, another milk can was found. A third milk can has not been found. Six thousand documents, more than thirty-five thousand pages, are now housed in the Jewish Historical Institute in Warsaw.

Examining the contents of the archives

A Banner Raised

In October 1942, fourteen-year-old Petr Ginz arrived from Prague at the Theresienstadt ghetto, lugging his twenty-pound suitcase. It was full of heavy winter clothing, with hundred-Mark bills sewn into jacket cuffs, as well as his treasured writing paper, watercolor paints, linoleum blocks, knives to cut the blocks, and his 260-page unfinished novel, *The Wizard of Altay Mountain*. His suitcase was too small for his four other completed novels.

Arriving at Theresienstadt, Czechoslovakia

In their continuing propaganda to convince the world that they were not mistreating Jews, the Nazis described Theresienstadt as a "model" ghetto, the "*Führer*'s gift to the Jews," a "spa town" for artists and intellectuals. The Germans had moved seven thousand Czech citizens out of Terezín and crammed fifty thousand Jews into this walled town forty miles from Prague. Like all new arrivals, Petr did not know that Theresienstadt was really a temporary stop on the way to death. The one Nazi truth about the ghetto was that thousands of Jewish artists, writers, musicians, and scientists were sent here.

Like all inmates fourteen and older, Petr worked mornings. Afternoons he attended secret classes in geography, history, math,

Petr Ginz

87

Background image:
Petr Ginz's painting of his
bunk at Theresienstadt

Hebrew, literature, and art. At night he attended lectures, concerts, and plays. Educators were determined that these Jewish youngsters, robbed of so much, would not be deprived of education. Secret ghetto libraries and schools kept the young occupied, gave them something to look forward to every day, and prepared them for their eventual return to normal life. Teachers taught Jewish history and traditions and opened their students' imaginations to create newspapers, poetry, and works of art. When the Germans learned what was going on in secret, they let the classes and performances continue, believing that they diverted people from thinking about their future.

The Nazis called the children's flea-ridden living quarters homes; Petr lived in Home One. His teacher, Valtr Eisinger, told his students about an autobiographical novel written by two Russian teenagers in an orphanage named Shkid. The students identified with the Russians, who had suffered many hardships. On the Sabbath night of December 11, 1942, the boys in Home One celebrated the creation of their imaginary republic of Shkid. Thirteen-year-old Walter Roth read Petr's proclamation of their defiance and determination to survive in their oppressive environment:

The banner has been raised. Home Number One has its own flag, the symbol of its future work and its future communal life. The Home has its own government. Why did we set it up? Because we no longer want to be an accidental group of boys, passively succumbing to the fate meted out to us. We want to create an active, mature society and through work and discipline transform our fate into a joyful, proud reality. [The Germans] have unjustly uprooted us from the soil that nurtured us. . . . They have only one aim in mind — to destroy us, not only physically but mentally and morally as well. Will they succeed? Never! Robbed of the sources of our culture, we shall create new ones. . . . We shall build a new and joyously triumphant life! Cut off from a well-ordered society, we shall create a new life together, based on organization, voluntary discipline and mutual trust.

Torn from our people by this terrible evil, we shall not allow our hearts to be hardened by hatred and anger, but today and forever, our highest aim shall be love for our fellow men, and contempt for racial, religious and nationalist strife.

Home One also created a secret magazine called *Vedem.* The name means "in the lead" or "the vanguard," referring to their group being in the first room in the first dormitory. *Vedem*'s symbols were a Jules Verne–style spaceship and star, which represented the future, and a book, which stood for learning. More than one hundred boys wrote and illustrated poetry, interviews, jokes, book reviews, stories, and articles. Every week, from December 18, 1942, to July 9, 1944, Petr edited and handwrote the only copy of each edition. When he wasn't reminding or hounding his staff to meet their weekly deadlines, he could be found, pens and pencils scattered about him, cross-legged in his lower bunk, correcting spelling and grammar. Every Friday night, on the Sabbath, the boys in Home One gathered to read aloud from their magazine.

Vedem, issue #52, December 27, 1943

Drawings by the Children of Theresienstadt

Passover Seder by Doris Weiserová

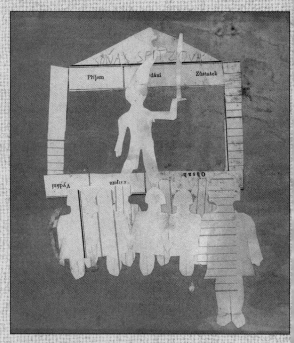

Guard with Stick by Soňa Spitzová

Study of Leaves by Milan Biennenfeld

Collage by Marta Kendeová

90

Aquarelle by Kitty Brunnerová

View of Terezín by Hans Weinberg

Vase with Flowers by Erika Stránská

Terezín Motif by Margit Gerstmannová

91

Pressed by the international community to see life in Theresienstadt firsthand, the Nazis finally allowed the Red Cross to visit in June 1944. Six months before the visit, the Nazis ordered the Jews to make improvements in the ghetto. *Vedem* reporters Hanus Weil and František Feuerstein recorded the elaborate Nazi charade, which succeeded in fooling the visitors.

SENSATION, SENSATION!!

On the day of the visit a large bun and unlimited quantities of coffee with milk and sugar are to be issued during the morning. There will be . . . a double portion of meat and potatoes for lunch, and in the evening, dumplings with sweet sauce. . . .

The Garrison Headquarters have ordered an intensive [beautification drive]. . . . On the day of arrival perfect order must be maintained from half-past eight onwards. For this purpose permission has been given to air, shake out and beat comforters, blankets, mattresses, etc. throughout the preceding day.

The cast of *Brundibár*

Red Cross officials were particularly charmed by a performance of the children's opera *Brundibár*. The visitors did not grasp the symbolism of its plot about a brother and sister who triumph over an evil organ grinder. Rudi Lauf, who appeared in the opera, described the premiere in *Vedem*.

As soon as the audience started filing in, our little souls were slowly but surely overcome by stage fright. . . . But as soon as the first bars of music sounded, we forgot our fear and went to it. . . . And when we had finished and the hall was filled with thunderous applause, we were all happy and content, for man is a creature eager for fame. And in all of us there was some satisfaction at having done a thing well. . . . Brundibár will soon disappear from the thoughts of those who watched it in Terezín, but for us actors it will remain one of the few beautiful memories we have of that place.

Only fifteen boys of the one hundred who passed through Home One survived. Petr Ginz was deported to Auschwitz on October 22, 1944, and sent directly to the gas chambers. *Vedem* contributor Zdeněk Taussig hid the magazines in the blacksmith shop where his father worked and retrieved them after the war.

THE ART TEACHER

When artist-teacher Friedl Dicker-Brandeis packed for Theresienstadt, she brought art supplies for children instead of articles for her personal needs. Almost two years later, before

being deported to Auschwitz, she stashed forty-five hundred children's drawings and paintings in two suitcases in the attic of one of the dormitories, leaving an indelible record of her students' memories, fantasies, imaginations, and emotions.

Friedl Dicker-Brandeis

"Resist to Our Last Breath"

VILNA GHETTO, OCCUPIED LITHUANIA

Twenty-three-year-old Abba Kovner listened intently to the eleven-year-old girl's trembling voice as she told her chilling story. In October 1941, Sara Menkes was among five thousand Jews who were rounded up in the Vilna ghetto in Lithuania and told they would be "resettled in the East." Instead, in groups of one hundred, the *Einsatzgruppen* and Lithuanian militia marched them off to prepared funeral pits in the Ponar forest four miles from the city. When the Soviets controlled the area, they had dug the pits for fuel storage. When the Germans attacked, the Soviets retreated and left the project uncompleted. At the pits the Jews were forced to undress, ordered to climb down into the pits, and sprayed with machine-gun fire.

Blindfolded Jews are marched to their deaths in the Ponar pits, 1941

Miraculously, the bullets missed Sara. For hours she stayed motionless. When all was quiet, she pushed her way up through the bodies and climbed out of the pit. Jews wandering about the forest found her naked under a bush. They brought her back to the ghetto, where she told her story to Jacob Gens, the head of the Jewish Council. Gens refused to believe her. He insisted that the Germans would never massacre Vilna's Jews; they desperately needed them to build weapons and make coats for their soldiers. Resettlement could not possibly be a lie. He warned

Sara that if she wanted her father to keep his work permit and stay alive, she'd best keep her silence.

But Abba Kovner knew that Sara Menkes spoke the truth. He believed that this massacre was only one small part of Hitler's plan to murder all of Europe's Jews. An underground fighting force had to be formed as quickly as possible and be ready should another march to the death pits be forced on the Jews. In the next six months, while twenty-year-old Ruzka Korczak recruited among Vilna's youths, more than forty-eight thousand Jews from nearby towns were executed at the Ponar pits.

On December 31, Korczak's recruits braved the snow and the Nazi curfew to hear Kovner speak at a secret meeting in the ghetto's public soup kitchen at 2 Strashun Street:

Jews in the Ponar pits, ca. June–July 1941

Abba Kovner

Let us not go like sheep to the slaughter, Jewish youth! Do not believe those who are deceiving you. Out of eighty thousand Jews of the Jerusalem of Lithuania, only twenty thousand remain. In front of your eyes our parents, our brothers and our sisters are being torn away from us. Where are the hundreds of men who were snatched away for labor by the Lithuanian kidnappers? Where are those naked women who were taken away on the horror-night of the provocation? Where are those Jews of the Day of Atonement? And where are our brothers of the second ghetto? Anyone who is taken out through the gates of the ghetto will never return.

Background image: Glaziers Street, former Vilna ghetto, postwar Poland

All roads of the ghetto lead to Ponar, and Ponar means death. Oh, despairing people — tear this deception away from your eyes. Your children, your husbands, your wives — are no longer alive — Ponar is not a labor camp. Everyone there is shot. Hitler aimed at destroying the Jews of Europe. It turned out to be the fate of the Jews of Lithuania to be the first.

Let us not go like sheep to the slaughter. It is true that we are weak, lacking protection, but the only reply to a murderer is resistance. Brothers, it is better to die as free fighters than to live at the mercy of killers. Resist, resist, to our last breath.

His words moved his young audience to tears.

Kovner immediately sent couriers to deliver his manifesto to other ghettos in Poland, in the hope of alerting Jews to the truth and inspiring them to form their own resistance units.

Three weeks later, on January 21, 1942, various factions in the Vilna ghetto united to form the United Partisans Organization (FPO). Yitzhak Wittenberg, a forty-year-old Jewish communist, became the leader. Zionists Kovner and twenty-nine-year-old Josef Glazman became his lieutenants.

For the next eighteen months, there were no more massacres: the ground was too frozen to dig new graves or to cover bodies, and the German army was preoccupied with fighting on the Russian front. But the FPO, knowing the Germans might strike at any time, met in secret at their headquarters to prepare. Two battalions were formed. Each battalion had six or eight platoons; each platoon had three squads; each squad had five fighters. Each group had a commander. All commanders took orders from Wittenberg. As in all underground groups, secrecy

Yitzhak Wittenberg

was critical. Not even family members were allowed to know that someone belonged to the FPO.

Weapons and ammunition were bought at exorbitant prices from Lithuanian police. Jews forced to repair German weapons smuggled arms parts into the ghetto. Unbeknownst to the Jewish Council, FPO members were on the Jewish police force. Any time Elchanan Telerant wore a black leather coat returning from work, it signaled his comrades in the Jewish police that he was smuggling in weapons, and they distracted the Lithuanian guards from searching him. The arms were hidden in the ghetto library, the Jewish cemetery, apartment walls, wells, and water buckets. The partisan units met in the library basement. They learned how to make grenades from old lightbulbs and held target practice with unloaded guns. Strategies were created for distributing weapons and getting fighters to their posts quickly. Shmuel Kaplinski, a sanitation engineer, spent weeks underground mapping out the sewer tunnels to smuggle in weapons and, if need be, for an escape route.

By the fall of 1942, almost two hundred young people had joined the FPO. Individuals, some who were members of the FPO and some who were not, conducted their own guerrilla actions. A postal worker destroyed thousands of letters destined for German soldiers and distributed food parcels meant for them to Jews. Jews assembling and packing bicycles for use by the German army cut through six hundred frames. Technicians in repair shops damaged sights in anti-aircraft guns, drilled holes in airplane fuel tanks, and removed essential parts from other equipment to cause malfunctioning. Jewish fur workers set fire to sixty thousand sheepskin coats intended for German soldiers freezing to death at the front. Three

Josef Glazman, July 5, 1934

One of the gates to the Vilna ghetto

hundred barrels of gasoline were torched in a fuel depot. Two brothers lost their lives blowing up an ammunition dump.

In July 1943, Kovner ordered Vitka Kempner to carry out the FPO's first mission: blowing up a German military transport. Kempner sneaked out of the ghetto and spent three days scouting the railroad tracks near the city. About four miles southeast of Vilna, she found a section of track on a trestle over a gorge. The next moonless night, she took two other partisans with her. She tied a pipe packed with dynamite to the track, laid a fuse along the rail, set it, and then returned to

Vilna. The next day an underground Polish newspaper attributed to Polish partisans the destruction of a train carrying two hundred German soldiers.

But triumph was short-lived. A month later, Jewish Council head Jacob Gens figured out that Josef Glazman, his deputy police officer, belonged to the FPO. Glazman and twenty others fled to the forest to set up a partisan base and from there fight the Germans with guerilla warfare.

A month after that, the Gestapo learned that Wittenberg was the head of the FPO and demanded that Gens deliver him to them. If Gens failed to do so, the Nazis threatened, they would bomb the ghetto and set it afire. Wittenberg went into hiding. Gens warned ghetto residents that they would be saved only if Wittenberg turned himself in. Most Jews in the ghetto did not support armed resistance. They still believed that they had a chance to survive if they could just hold out until the war ended. Outraged, they stormed through the streets to FPO headquarters and demanded Wittenberg's surrender. Wittenberg knew that the ghetto and all the Jews in it would be destroyed sooner or later, but he did not want to be the person responsible for hastening that fate. He turned himself in and committed suicide by swallowing a cyanide capsule. Twenty-three-year-old Abba Kovner was now in charge.

The Nazi web of deception continued. Vilna's Jews were told they could be relocated to the ghetto in Kovno (today called Kaunas). Four hundred Jews, who believed what the Nazis said, packed their suitcases and ended up at the Ponar death pits.

Left to right: Vitka Kempner, Ruzka Korczak, Zelda Traeger

By August 1943, the FPO had more than three hundred members. A second partisan group, the Yechiel Struggle Group, had two hundred. But only thirteen thousand Jews out of eighty thousand were left in Vilna. The Nazis closed all the workshops and factories outside the ghetto except for the fur factory and announced that three thousand "volunteers" were needed to work in Estonia's labor camps. When those numbers were met, they demanded another five thousand. This time no one volunteered.

At dawn on Wednesday, September 1, German soldiers stomped through the ghetto to round up Jews for the work camps. A skirmish broke out between a group of Vilna partisans and the Germans. Kovner knew this was the moment to fight. He sent couriers through the ghetto to deliver a manifesto urging every Jew to take up arms.

Jews! Defend yourselves with arms. The German and Estonian hangmen have arrived at the gates of the ghetto. They have come to murder us! Within a short while, they will lead us, group after group, through the gate. Thus they led our brothers and sisters, our mothers and fathers, our children. Thus were tens of thousands taken out to their death! But we shall not go! . . . We have nothing to lose, death will take us in any event. . . . Only armed resistance can save our lives and honor. Brothers! Better to fall in battle than to be led like sheep to the slaughter. . . . There is an organized Jewish resistance in the ghetto that will rise with arms. Lend a hand to the revolt. . . . Whoever has no weapons, take a hatchet; and whoever has no hatchet, take a pipe or a stick. For our fathers! For our murdered children! . . . Strike at the dogs. . . . We have nothing to lose! Death to the murderers!

When Vilna's Jews did not answer the call, Kovner knew that there was no point in staying. It was time to join the partisans in the Rudnicki forest twelve miles away. He sent two women ahead to find a safe route.

They would escape the ghetto through the sewer system. Recent rains had raised the water level so much that only twenty or thirty people could go underground at one time, for too many bodies would cause the water to rise above their heads. It was raining now, and Kovner knew if the rain got more ferocious, they would surely drown underground.

Shmuel Kaplinski suggested a new route that ended outside the ghetto two miles away in the yard of the German Security Police. Too dangerous, Kovner argued. Kaplinski disagreed: it was the perfect place, because the Germans would never suspect that the Jews would be so foolish as to come there. The underground journey would take six hours.

Kovner went to tell his mother that he was leaving. He explained that getting through the sewers would be extremely difficult, even for the young. Only trained fighters were allowed to go. "What will become of me?" she asked. He had no answer. His decision to leave her, abandoning her to die alone, was to haunt him the rest of his life.

Shmuel Kaplinski, Vilna, Lithuania

Left to right: Ruzka Korczak, Abba Kovner, and Vitka Kempner during the liberation of Vilna

As Ruzka Korczak descended the ladder into the sewer, she heard the distant echo of feet overhead as the remaining Jews in the ghetto were rounded up. Kovner followed behind. Ammonia and sulfur filled her nostrils as she touched the bottom rung of the ladder. She tried not to choke. She could barely see ahead. A miner's lamp provided the only light in this dark underground of muck. When the person holding the lamp turned a corner, it was pitch black.

She felt water around her legs. Heavy rain was coming in through the tunnel roof and grates. Would the water rise enough to drown them? The height of the tunnel roofs varied greatly. Korczak was only five feet tall, but there were sections where the ceilings were so low that she had to crawl. Some paths were no wider than her shoulders. Her hands and coat sleeves became coated with muck and slime. What if her weapon got wet and became useless? She felt every jerk of fear from the person ahead. People moaned and sobbed and called out their own names as if to confirm that they were still alive. Some fainted from the foul air and were dragged along to where an open grate brought in some fresh air. A few times, Korczak fell behind. Every time, Abba touched her back: "You will make it, Ruzka," he encouraged her.

As they passed outside the ghetto into the Christian part of Vilna, she heard water overhead as people washed their dinner dishes and flushed their toilets. Shmuel Kaplinski had said the trip would take six hours. Could she make it? Her legs felt as if they would crumble. Her slime-covered fingers were numb as she touched the walls along the way. Finally she came to the ladder leading out of the sewer. She grabbed its sides and climbed unsteadily into the fresh air. The rain, so threatening below, now felt magical on her face. She looked up and saw Vitka's warm smile. She saw Shmuel leaning against a stone wall. She turned back and saw Abba right behind her.

Kovner divided the group in two. One half paired off as couples and walked to the fur factory, where Kempner had arranged for them to hide. Kovner's group of fifteen slipped into the cellar of the German Security Police building. They huddled together in silence, listening to the sounds of the Germans overhead. Would they be discovered?

Two days passed. Kovner had studied a map of the villages nearby but was uncertain if he could lead the group through the woods and find the partisan camp. But it was too dangerous to stay any longer. When night fell, the FPO fighters sneaked up the stairs and out the side door of the building. It was raining hard. They paired off, talking and laughing, as they walked through the Christian part of Vilna, trying to act natural, like any locals, and hoping no one would notice their dirty clothes and faces. They came to a bridge that was usually guarded, but the guards had abandoned their posts in the downpour. They crossed the bridge and waited out the rain in a cave a few miles away. The next morning, desperately hungry, they stole chickens and roasted them. On the third day, they came across the body of one of the women scouts. She had been murdered.

Background image:
Street scene, prewar Vilna

For three weeks, they picked their way through dark swamps and ravines. Finally, signs nailed to tree trunks warned that they were in partisan territory, but where was the partisan camp? Approaching a swamp, they saw rising smoke. Could it be from a partisan campfire? Kovner sent Kempner and two others ahead to find a path around the swamp. After eight hours of fighting off mosquitoes, sinking into mud, and wading through water up to their necks, they found a log bridge crossing the swamp.

They went back to get the others. When the whole group finally crossed the swamp, they found themselves surrounded by rifles. Would they be killed now, after having come so far?

"It's Abba," a man's voice called out.

They were among their own again, temporarily safe.

Partisans near a hut they built, Rudnicki forest, Poland

Partisans on the day of Vilna's liberation, including Abba Kovner (back row center), Ruzka Korczak (third from right), and Vitka Kempner (far right)

Henrik Zimanas, a former Soviet commander, was head of partisan units in the southern part of Lithuania. Known by his underground name, Yurgis, Zimanas arrived as the Vilna partisans were almost finished building their camp. He informed Kovner that his fighters could not stay together; they would have to be split up and reassigned to other groups. He also told Kovner that the women could not be fighters and would have to live in a family camp. Kovner understood that the reason for mixed partisan units was to make the Jews less visible: Lithuanian partisans and Polish Home Army units had carried their anti-Semitism into the forest. Nevertheless Kovner refused both orders, telling Zimanas that the women had already proven they were as courageous and tenacious as any man. He argued that Jews must fight as Jews. He reminded Zimanas that the Lithuanians had not come to their rescue in the ghettos and that many had even tormented and murdered Jews. How could he ask his fighters to hide among them, to split off from the only people they could trust? Zimanas acquiesced.

As more Jews escaped from Vilna, the Kovno ghetto, and other nearby ghettos, Jewish partisan units in the forest grew. Like other partisans, they harassed, sabotaged, and fought the Germans until the war ended. Abba Kovner and Vitka Kempner married. They and Ruzka Korczak lived out the rest of their lives in the *Kibbutz Ein Hahoresh,* in Israel.

PART FOUR
IN THE CAMPS

During the cold nights
And until dawn
We sigh, plunged into our dreams of happiness
The sweet dreams die at dawn
Oh! If it were possible for one to die also.

We leave with plows and picks
We march, we march
Birds with amputated wings
With hearts bitter like bile.

In Leptokaria we dig, we dig
A soil — hard, ungrateful
The tenacious hunger gnaws us.
She buried her children.

— Maurice Chaim, labor camp, Leptokaria, occupied Greece, age and date unknown

Jews await deportation,
Rivesaltes transit camp, France

TRANSIT CAMPS

In Holland, France, Belgium, Italy, and Greece, Jews were rounded up and sent to internment or transit camps. From these temporary holding stations, Jews were deported to their deaths.

The Germans divided France into two major zones. The northern and northwestern parts of France were under German military control. The Nazis appointed Marshal Philippe Pétain, an eighty-four-year-old French hero of World War I, to govern the so-called unoccupied or free zone in south-central France, with headquarters in Vichy. Pétain cooperated fully with the Germans. Germany's ally Italy was given control over the part of France bordering their country. There were no internment or transit camps in the Italian zone.

In August 1941, Drancy, in the northeastern suburb of Paris, became an internment camp for foreign Jews. It later became the major transit camp for deporting all Jews living in France, including its own citizens. From June 22, 1942, until July 31, 1944, a total of 64,759 Jews were deported from Drancy to extermination camps: approximately 61,000 to Auschwitz-Birkenau and 3,753 to Sobibor. Fully one-third were French citizens.

Background image:
Barrack 51, Westerbork transit
camp, the Netherlands

108

In October 1939, the Dutch government established a camp at Westerbork, located in the northeastern Netherlands, for German Jews who had illegally entered the country. In late 1941, the Germans turned it into a transit camp. From July 1942 through September 1944 almost 100,000 Jews passed through Westerbork going to Bergen-Belsen, the Theresienstadt ghetto, Auschwitz-Birkenau, and Sobibor. Fewer than 5,000 Jewish deportees survived the war.

In Belgium, Jews were sent to Mechelen, a transit center in a former army barracks, located halfway between Antwerp and Brussels. Between August 1942 and July 1944, more than 25,000 Jews from Belgium were deported to Auschwitz-Birkenau via Mechelen.

A policeman directs women and children in the Rivesaltes transit camp, France, September 4, 1942

The Ambush

Hertz Jospa was fiercely proud of his Jewish comrades. Jews were resisting on all fronts. They had joined with non-Jews in Belgium's national resistance organization, the *Front de l'Indépendance.* They had formed the Jewish Defense Committee (CDJ) and were rescuing children. Jews also belonged to the Belgian Partisan Army, whose forte was sabotage. In one incident, its members dynamited a German army warehouse containing straw and cattle feed. In another, it attacked and raided a police station, making off with sixty-two thousand food ration cards and twenty-four pistols.

Hertz Jospa

Nine months earlier, Nazi officials told the Jewish Council in Brussels that one thousand Jews a week were expected to "volunteer" to work in labor camps for the German war effort. Most Jews were taken in by the lie that they were being resettled. They thought that by cooperating, they would save themselves and their families.

Jospa's comrades saw through the lie to the real agenda: foreign-born Jews in Belgium were to be deported, voluntarily or involuntarily, to their deaths. Jewish partisans went door-to-door, warning people and urging them to go into hiding instead.

Nevertheless, the Jewish Council followed the German order — out of either fear or ignorance — and drew up deportation lists with people's names and addresses. Jewish partisans, disguised in SS uniforms, broke into the council's headquarters and burned the registration

Vans deliver Jews to the Mechelen transit camp, Belgium

cards and lists. Unfortunately, there were duplicates. Outraged, the partisans assassinated the Jewish Council member who had prepared the lists.

But the powerful Nazi machine could not be stopped. There had already been nineteen transports since the previous July and

18,492 Jews deported. Still, Jospa felt there was some hope of rescuing others. Recently, sixty-four people, led by resistance fighters, had jumped out of the windows of a passenger-train transport while the guards were sleeping. Their actions encouraged Jospa to think that others could try to escape from the next transport.

Why not ambush it? It would be completely unexpected. In the confusion and surprise, the resisters could open the boxcar doors and help the prisoners out. The transports usually left at night, so darkness would be an ally. The escapees would need money, but the American Jewish Joint Distribution Committee had been sending 750,000 Belgian francs (more than $17,000) a month to feed Jews in hiding. Surely the Joint would send money for these escapees, too. Couriers could be sent across the border into Switzerland to ask for the money.

Jospa believed his idea was sound, but when he shared it with his comrades, they said it was impossible. Each transport had at least seventeen boxcars. Twenty or more armed men would be needed to attack both the front and back of the transport. They simply didn't have enough people or weaponry to do that. Many of their best fighters had been rounded up. More than two hundred had been executed.

Finally, once freed, how would the Jews get away? Each transport held at least a thousand people. Every inch of the area would be searched for the escapees. It was unrealistic to think that people living near the scene of the attack could or would hide that many people. The resistance had no vehicles. No, their organization wasn't equipped for this kind of action. They were saboteurs. They burned warehouses. They killed Germans and collaborators. They acted swiftly and then fled.

Jospa listened to their objections, but the notion of stopping the next transport had taken hold of him and wouldn't let go. He shared his thoughts with Youra Livchitz, a twenty-five-year-old Jewish doctor whose brother and mother were involved in resistance activities.

Livchitz agreed that it was imperative to try to stop this transport. But when he spoke to his friends, most repeated what Jospa's comrades had said: the plan was too dangerous, and they were not equipped for such an action. But two non-Jews, Jean Franklemon and Robert Maistriau, agreed to help.

Youra Livchitz

Jean Franklemon

Robert Maistriau

Independent of the plans beginning in Brussels to ambush the next transport, Jews imprisoned in the transit center of Mechelen were plotting their own escapes. Mechelen, a former army barracks, was disguised from the outside by basalt doors decorated with the inscription THE HAPSBURG COURT, as if it were a royal building.

As in all ghettos and camps, Mechelen had an active underground. Albert Clement, a Jewish maintenance worker, was often sent to town with a guard to buy supplies. Many times the hardware-store owner slipped an extra tool or two into his bundle while the guard wasn't looking. While making repairs around the camp, Clement hid nails and screws and tools for the inmates to use. One morning when prisoners were washing, two faucets above the washbasins burst. Cold water blasted out of the wall. Clement was rushed off to town to buy new faucets. He returned with a bundle of fifty-franc notes slipped to him by the hardware-store owner.

On his many rounds of the camp, he talked to various prisoners, learned who was planning to escape, and gave out the money.

Meanwhile, Jacques Cyngiser, a member of the Jewish resistance, convinced Eva Fastag, a Jewish secretary in the camp's SS office, to give consecutive numbers to the resistance prisoners being deported so they would be put together in one boxcar. Eva carefully arranged the lists: Abraham Fischel, 1360; Nathan Mitelsbach, 1362; Jacques Cyngiser, 1366; Icek Wolman, 1369; Symcha Weberman, 1379; Abraham Bloder, 1380; Majer Tabakman, 1381.

A Jewish prisoner was assigned to guard every boxcar to make sure people behaved. The guards were given small yellow flags and ordered to wave them out of the barred window if anyone died or tried to escape. Eva Fastag got Cyngiser appointed as a guard.

Abraham Bloder found scraps of cigarette paper among the dried macaroni in a food parcel sent by friends. He carefully pieced the fragments together and read the message saying that the resistance was planning to stop the next transport. The news boosted his morale and determination. Bloder stuffed his suitcase with pliers and saws sharpened by workers in the metal shop. Jacques Grauwels smuggled a small saw out of the metal shop.

Escape was the daily preoccupation of Regine Krochmal, an eighteen-year-old nurse. The idea of escaping touched even the young: eleven-year-old Simon Gronowski practiced jumping down from his top bunk so he could jump the four feet off the train.

Simon Gronowski (age 11) and his parents, Brussels, 1942

As these prisoners plotted their escapes, Youra Livchitz and his comrades Jean Franklemon and Robert Maistriau searched for the right place to attack the transport. It had to be outside Brussels, where there were fewer houses, yet still within biking distance of the city and close enough to public transportation so that people could return to their hometowns to hide. On a map, Livchitz located a forest just beyond the Boortmeerbeek rail station about fifteen miles from Brussels. People could hide in the woods until the morning tram to Brussels came.

He bicycled out to the area and found a bend in the rail route not too far from the train station. The spot seemed perfect. They would place a red emergency signal here. Rounding the curve, the engineer would naturally slow down and stop when he saw the red light. As a group, rail workers had shown strong resistance to the Germans. Livchitz had heard that on more than one occasion, an engineer had deliberately slowed a transport so that people could jump off.

A sympathetic member of the Jewish Council informed Jospa that the transport would leave Mechelen around ten p.m., traveling thirty miles an hour. Livchitz calculated it would reach the spot he had chosen when it was still dark.

On the evening of April 19, Livchitz, Franklemon, and Maistriau arrived at the chosen spot, carrying bundles of fifty-franc notes. At the bend in the tracks, Maistriau placed a hurricane lamp with red tissue paper glued to the glass. He lit it. It looked like a real emergency signal. He was sure the engineer would think so, too, and stop the train when he saw it.

Livchitz took up his position close to where he believed the first car would stop. Previous transports had had only one armed guard at the front. Livchitz hoped that his revolver could fend off that guard. Maistriau walked to what he believed would be the middle of the six-hundred-foot-long transport; Franklemon walked toward the end. They planned to meet an hour after the attack.

What the three men did not know was that this transport was unlike previous ones: the Germans had replaced the passenger cars with windowless cattle cars bolted shut from the outside.

Early on April 19, 1943, the Jewish prisoners were made to line up. As on all previous transports, prisoners had to wear their numbers on pieces of cardboard hanging around their necks. It took from early morning until ten p.m. to load and lock the 1,631 Jews, including 262 children,

Detainees of the 8th transport are humiliated while awaiting deportation from Mechelen transit camp to Auschwitz, September 1942

into thirty boxcars. Eighteen-year-old Jacques Grauwels used that time to saw through the bars of a hatch. In another car, Joseph Silber sawed an opening in the wall. In still another car, Jacques Cyngiser drilled a hole large enough to reach through and open the lock on the sliding door from the outside.

Regine Krochmal was assigned as a guard on the "medical" car, a label she thought absurd considering there was no water or medicine for the sick. Right before she was to board, the Jewish doctor in charge of Mechelen's medical wing slipped her a long knife and whispered, "Make sure you can escape. You are destined to be gassed and burned." She didn't believe what the doctor had said; it was unimaginable. But she did believe that conditions at the concentration camp would be so horrendous that the sick and elderly would not survive. She tucked the knife into an inside pocket of her cloak.

As the transport pulled away from Mechelen, Krochmal told the young doctor assigned to her car that she was planning to escape. She urged him to join her, but he said he could not abandon his patients. She looked at the frail men and women lying on straw. She insisted his loyalty was admirable but pointless. He had no medicine to help anyone. Most likely these people would not survive the trip. Still she could not convince him. There was no more time to waste. She began sawing the pine bars on the windows. They gave way easily. She tried to reach the hatch on the side of the boxcar. She was too short, so she stood on a suitcase. More luck. The nails holding the hatch also came off without any effort. She pushed it open and slipped out feetfirst. She twisted her body and grabbed the top of the hatch with her fingers. Now, if the transport would only slow down. And as if she had commanded it, it did. She pressed her feet against the boxcar wall, released her grip on the hatch, and fell to the ground.

At almost the same time, Jacques Cyngiser had successfully unbolted his boxcar door. One by one, the men in his car jumped out.

As the transport rattled on past Krochmal, she picked herself up from the ground and looked up. The clouds were moving fast across the sky. The moon was full. A guard looking out one of the windows might see her. She had to get to the cover of the forest quickly.

Simon Gronowski's mother shook him from sleep. When he opened his eyes, he saw people jumping out of the open car. His mother held on to the shoulder of his jacket while he grabbed a bar on the right side of the car. He sat down, his feet dangling out of the boxcar. "Don't jump yet," she warned. "The train is going too fast."

When he felt it slow, he shouted, "I'm jumping now!"

As he landed on the ground, he heard machine-gun fire and men shouting in German. He looked back at the train, belching white smoke into the sky. He didn't see his mother. Hadn't she jumped? Was she still inside the boxcar? He wanted to stay and find out, but he knew he might be shot if he lingered, so he ran into the dark forest.

Hidden in the forest, Robert Maistriau listened for the locomotive whistle. When he finally spotted thick clouds of steam rising into the sky, he knew the train was close. He heard its shrill whistle as it approached the bend in the tracks. What if the engineer didn't see the red lamp? What if he didn't stop the train? Robert silently prayed for their plan to work. Then he heard the sound of screeching brakes. The lamp had worked! The engineer had stopped the train!

He ran to the nearest car and frantically cut the barbed wire holding the door bolts. He opened the door and held up his little torch. "Leave, leave!" he shouted. People pushed and shoved and scrambled to get out. The wagon guard tried to block them. "It's forbidden," he said. "The Germans will shoot us all."

Maistriau heard pistol fire, which he assumed was from Youra's gun. The guards carried machine guns. He listened for a response. There was none. Their plan was working. The Germans were likely confused and didn't realize that there were only three of them and one revolver. He raced to the next car. By the time he got there, machine-gun fire was spraying all about him. Had the Germans figured it out? No time to wonder. He ran back into the forest. Seven people were waiting there. He distributed the fifty-franc notes and directed the escapees to the nearest train station. One woman hugged him. He watched them disappear into the forest and headed back to the meeting place.

Jean Franklemon was there. He described his narrow escape: Unlike past transports, this one had had police at the end, where he was stationed. He had barely cut through the boxcar wire when they had fired at him. He had raced into the forest, an officer at his heels, managing to knock the man out and get away.

Franklemon and Maistriau waited another half hour, but Livchitz never showed. They biked to Brussels, hoping he was safe.

Livchitz had had a narrow escape, too. When the engineer stopped the train, Livchitz fired his pistol. Two guards immediately came after him. As one drew close, Livchitz shot wildly at him. The shots seemed to scare the guard away, but Livchitz felt it would be too risky to go back to the meeting place to retrieve his bicycle, so he walked the fifteen miles back to Brussels. It took him eight hours.

When Regine Krochmal heard the transport screech to a halt, then the sound of gunfire, she did not wait around. She walked parallel to the railroad tracks until she came to a crossing guardhouse. Through the lighted window, she saw a young man reading. There was a chance he could be hostile, even a collaborator, but she had to risk it. She pushed open the door. "I've just escaped from a transport," she said. He put his finger to his mouth to silence her. In a meadow of haystacks behind the guardhouse, he spread bundled hay and she jumped into it. He smoothed it and returned to his post.

She heard the dogs barking before she heard the footsteps. Then she smelled cigarette smoke and heard two men speaking German. Her heart pounded. Would the dogs sniff the hay? Would the men probe the hay with their weapons? Minutes passed as if they were hours, until there were no more footsteps or cigarette smoke or voices. The crossing guard returned with food and directed her to the nearest tram station.

Robert Maistriau freed seventeen people. Two hundred thirty-one people unlocked the boxcar doors and jumped out, but ninety were recaptured. Twenty-six died trying to run away. One hundred fifteen succeeded in escaping, including Joseph Silber, Samuel Perl, Jacques Cyngiser, Jacques Grauwels, Regine Krochmal, and Simon Gronowski.

Grauwels and a friend arrived, wet and filthy, at a tram station and waited nervously for a tram. If the German soldiers on the platform spotted them, they would certainly ask to see their nonexistent papers. But without a word, workers waiting on the platform encircled the two young men so they would not be seen.

Simon Gronowski found his way to the nearby hamlet of Berlingen. Various families hid him until Belgium was liberated. Regine Krochmal was recaptured and taken back to Mechelen, where she remained until she was liberated on September 3, 1944. Hertz Jospa was arrested on June 21, 1943, and sent to Birkenau concentration camp. He survived the war and settled in London. Jean Franklemon and Robert Maistriau survived imprisonment in various concentration camps.

The Gestapo captured and executed Youra Livchitz.

Monument to the victims of deportation from Belgium and those who ambushed the 20th transport, Boortmeerbeek rail station, Belgium

LABOR CAMPS

Forced laborers haul dirt at Mauthausen concentration camp, Austria, 1942

When Germany attacked the Soviet Union in 1941, still more German men were drafted into the army, but Germany also needed people to produce food, weapons, and equipment for the war. The Germans looked to the occupied territories to meet the need. They exploited Jewish labor in ghettos, used concentration camp prisoners and prisoners of war, and created thousands of labor camps for Jews and non-Jews. They eventually forced millions of Europeans to work for them. At more than eleven thousand sites in labor camps and ghettos in German-occupied Europe, prisoners mined ore, dug peat, laid railroad tracks, sewed uniforms, grew food, repaired airplanes, and built bombs. They hauled bricks and lumber to build additional structures in concentration camps to house the ever-growing populations.

Most large concentration camps had satellite camps where Jews and non-Jews worked for private German companies that sought to profit from the seemingly endless supply of cheap labor. Auschwitz's 430-acre complex consisted of three main camps and forty satellite forced-labor camps where Jews worked in coal mines, chemical and munitions plants, and agricultural and forestry stations. Some labor camps, like the one in Novogrudok, Belorussia (now Belarus), were small.

Forced laborers weave baskets in Jasenovac labor camp, Yugoslavia

Child laborer, Kovno ghetto, Lithuania, ca. 1941–1944

Forced laborers sew German military uniforms in the Olkusz ghetto, Poland, 1942

Jewish women at forced labor on "Industry Street," Plaszow concentration camp, Poland

Three Feet a Day

NOVOGRUDOK LABOR CAMP, OCCUPIED BELORUSSIA

Idel Kagan

Fourteen-year-old Idel Kagan sat next to his father, stitching leather. Five hundred Jews in the camp produced fur coats, gloves, felt boots, overcoats, and saddles for the German army. How lucky that Idel's father knew the Polish foreman and had managed to get Idel transferred here. Stitching leather in this unheated workshop was certainly better than digging up heavy stones and carting them away in the bitter cold and rain. No longer could the cruel SS officer whip Idel if he didn't move the stones fast enough.

In the fourteen months since the Germans had marched triumphantly into Novogrudok, they had murdered almost six thousand Jews from Novogrudok and surrounding towns. Miraculously, Idel's parents, his sister, his uncle Notke, his aunt, and their daughter had so far been spared, along with five hundred other "skilled" workers in the labor camp. Another five hundred Jews were imprisoned in the ghetto. The Novogrudok labor camp had been set up in the former district courthouse complex. It was enclosed by two rows of barbed wire and a high wooden fence that prevented outsiders from seeing in. There was a police station on one side. Local police guarded the gates. Day and night, ten guards in the watchtowers focused machine guns and searchlights on the camp yard. Two buildings were used as workshops. Two sheds and a stable were living quarters. Idel slept on a three-tiered bunk with twenty other men in an unheated room with one window.

Idel Kagan (third from right) with cousins, including Berl, Novogroduk, 1936

Idel had learned that the Bielski brothers had organized a family camp in the Naliboki forest fifty miles away and that they welcomed all Jews to join them. Idel was acquainted with the youngest brother, Archik, from school. A dogcatcher, Franciszek Bobrowski, and a farmer, Konstantin Kozlowski, who lived nearby had opened their homes to serve as way stations for Jews trying to get to the Bielski encampment. Idel's cousin Berl had already run away. Idel was determined to follow him. His parents had given him their blessing to leave.

In late November, Idel's friend Ruvke Oppenheim sneaked back into the labor camp to lead his mother and sister out to the Bielski encampment. Idel studied Ruvke's every move. One snowy December day, he saw Ruvke

Ruvke Oppenheim

wearing a heavier jacket than usual — a sure sign that he was leaving.

So Idel donned his own wool gloves, a cap, and a pair of felt boots that he stole from one of the warehouses with the help of another prisoner. For added protection from the cold, he put paper bags that had once held cement under his jacket.

The snow was already waist high and still coming down heavily. That was good — it would soon cover his footprints. There were no guards or police at the gates. They never ventured outside in heavy snow. When the first supply truck of the day came through the open gates, Idel tore off his star and his identification number and walked out the camp gates across the road into the forest.

By afternoon, thirteen more escapees waited impatiently in the woods for dark so they could walk the six miles to Bobrowski's house. The temperature dropped. There was no wind that day, but Idel felt like he was breathing frozen air. With every step, he sank deeper. Chills shot through his body. The snow covered familiar landmarks, and the escapees were unaware when they reached a shallow, fast-moving part of the river. Its thin, icy crust cracked under Idel's feet. The freezing water soaked right through his felt boots and turned them to blocks of ice, a few inches thick all around. It was like walking on stilts made of bricks. Nevertheless he pushed one foot in front of the other, determined not to fall behind the others and to reach Bobrowski's hut.

They were late for the midnight rendezvous. The Bielski couriers, thinking no one was coming, had already left. Bobrowski said they wouldn't return for another three days. It was too dangerous for them to stay in his barn until then. Idel knew he would not survive outside. Already he couldn't feel his toes. Most likely they were frostbitten. He had no choice. He would have to return to the camp and try to escape another time. Hardly able to walk, he rolled down the snow-packed hill near Bobrowski's hut and lay waiting near the road, wondering how he would ever manage the six-mile trek back to the camp.

Luck was with him. A sled came by, the team of horses trudging through the thick snow. Idel managed to get up and throw himself onto its open back. The driver never noticed him. When the sled reached the water well just three hundred feet from the labor camp, Idel slid off and hunkered down in the snow. It was only a few more hours until dawn, only a few more hours until some prisoners were let out of the camp to get water from the well. They would help him sneak back into the camp. But first he had to stay awake so he wouldn't freeze to death.

The prisoner water brigade spotted Idel. The guards, wrapped from head to toe to fend off the bitter cold, never noticed him. Surrounded by inmates, Idel crawled back into the camp.

His iced-over felt boots were glued to his skin. In the unheated room, the ice would not melt. His father tried to cut the boots away, one small piece of felt at a time. Idel's black toes on both feet were indeed frostbitten. They would have to be amputated before gangrene set in and he lost both legs. Four days later, four men held Idel down on his bunk during the amputation. There were no painkillers, antiseptics, or even bandages in the camp. Someone stuffed a rag into his mouth to stifle his screams, but Idel never cried out in spite of the excruciating pain.

He lay on his bunk for eight months, recuperating, his thin body touching the wooden slats. He covered himself but was never warm.

Bedbugs crawled into the rags wrapped around his feet. He tried not to scratch, but it was impossible. So he scratched, and his wounds reopened, prolonging the healing process.

Idel's mother, Dvorah Kagan

Two months after Idel escaped, the electric station in Novogrudok stopped functioning and the Polish engineer there could not fix it. He suggested to the Germans that Ruvke Shabakovski, a Jewish forced laborer and a first-class engineer, might solve the problem, and he did. When the work was finished, the Pole asked the German guard for permission to reward Shabakovski with a half sack of flour. The guard agreed, as Shabakovski had worked hard. Once back in the camp, Ruvke discovered a small radio hidden inside the sack. One man was put in charge of listening to the news.

On February 4, 1943, the radio brought the glorious news that the Soviets had defeated the Germans at Stalingrad two days earlier in the largest battle of the war. But the same day brought word that the five hundred remaining Jews in the Novogrudok ghetto had been murdered. In May, Idel's mother, sister, and an aunt were among 228 Jews killed in another round of shootings in the labor camp. As far as Idel knew, his father, his uncle Notke, and his cousin Berl, if he was still alive, were his only surviving relatives.

The 250 Jews left in the labor camp, knowing they would soon be murdered, formed an escape committee. Idel's uncle Notke was on the committee, which met in Idel's room. Idel listened as various plans were debated, including a mass breakout and armed uprising. They didn't have enough weapons and knew they wouldn't be able to get many

Ladder into the
tunnel, Novogrudok
labor camp

more. Bribes to the local police so far had bought only six rifles, a few
pistols, and two hand grenades.

They settled on digging a tunnel to the middle of a wheat field 328
feet on the other side of the barbed wire. They would start the tunnel
under the bunk beds in the living quarters farthest from the guards' station. The SS never went there for fear of disease, a reasonable fear given
the appalling conditions under which the Jews were forced to live. Every
Jew in camp, except for an Austrian suspected of being an informer, was
told about the plan.

Berl Yoselevitz, an engineer, worked out the measurements: the
tunnel would be five feet below the ground, two feet across, and thirty
inches high, just big enough for one person to crawl through at a time. If

they started at the beginning of May and dug at a rate of three feet a day, they could reach the wheat field by the middle of August. By then the wheat would be four feet tall and provide cover as they emerged from the tunnel and ran into the forest. The only question was whether they would be alive long enough to complete the tunnel.

A lower bunk bed was detached and rehinged so it could be pulled up and down quickly. Assignments were given: the metalworkers made funnels and small shovels from scraps of metal and resharpened the tools every day; the carpenters built a trolley track and a trolley with hinges on the sides so dirt could be pushed into the open side. When the trolley was full, the flaps would be closed. People gave up their blankets, and the tailors made sixty sacks for holding the dirt. Idel's father made the leather reins to pull the trolley.

Digging finally commenced in mid-May. During the day, only one man dug at a time so he would not be as likely to be missed at work. Carefully, slowly, the diggers crawled on their naked bellies, scooping up earth. Every six feet, they pierced the tunnel roof with a stick to make sure it would not cave in. Engineer Yoselevitz constantly checked that they were digging in a straight line.

At night, Idel dragged his weakened body to join the living conveyor belt of men and women passing the dirt sacks out of the tunnel, into their living quarters, and up a ladder to a loft.

As they dug farther, oxygen grew scarcer. There wasn't enough air to burn an oil lamp. The metalworkers made cone-shaped pipes to bring in air through the tunnel roof. They also widened the tunnel for better air flow, but the oil lamps still struggled to stay lit.

Avram Rukovski, a master electrician, scavenged old wires and stole some electric bulbs from his workshop and jerry-rigged a switchboard that controlled the camp's searchlights. To get light in the tunnel, he diverted electricity from the main switchboard, which caused a power failure. With the first power failure, the commandant called upon Rukovski to figure out what was wrong. Rukovski insisted he couldn't find anything wrong. A Polish electrician was called in, but he could not find the source of the problem either. The Nazis came to accept the frequent, short power failures as normal, a mere nuisance.

Holes were made in the ceiling so that the prisoners could communicate and to let the stale air out. The dug-out earth was piled on both sides of the loft. When the loft was full, double walls were built. Dirt was also buried under floorboards. They ran out of places to hide the dirt. They mixed it with the garbage, and on Sundays, cleaning day, they dumped it into the well. It clogged the well. The Germans ordered them to clean the well. It got clogged again. They cleaned it again. The Germans couldn't understand why the well constantly clogged.

Idel's father, Yankiel Kagan

The Jews got permission to dig new toilets and filled part of the trenches with tunnel dirt. Idel thought it magic that the Nazis had no idea what was really going on.

Rain came. The tunnel roof began to sink. Bunk beds were taken apart to prop it up. The tunnel walls began to crack. More wood was stolen to brace them.

In early July, Idel's father was sent to Koldichevo, known to be the worst labor camp in the area. Idel wondered if he would ever see his father again.

In August the tunnel was almost complete, but then the wheat was harvested. Everyone feared that the weight of the tractor might cause the tunnel roof to collapse. It didn't. But with the wheat cut, the tunnel would now exit into an open field. There was more digging to be done so that the tunnel would exit near a small hill, where they were less likely to be detected when they emerged.

Finally, toward the end of September, the tunnel was ready. Idel's wounds had healed enough for him to practice walking. Despite excruciating pain, he managed to walk to a small mirror in his room. Was this skinny boy with the long, unruly hair really he? He looked down at his matchstick legs. Would he be able to make it through the tunnel? And if he did, would he have the strength to walk the distance to the Bielski camp? He was determined to try. Whatever happened, he would not let the Germans take him alive. He was allowed to make a trial run through the tunnel. His confidence surged when he crawled to the end and back without stopping.

Idel Kagan (left) and Tevele
Niankovski, 1944

Eighteen-year-old Pesach Abramowitz, who had also tried to escape the previous December, had suffered frostbite, too, and lost the toes on one foot. He was still limping badly, but he was as determined as Idel to make it through the tunnel. They decided to team up.

As he had last December, Idel prepared for the escape. He traded his father's woolen coat for a pair of warm pants and two pieces of bread. He stole a pistol holster and belt from the saddle-making workshop, hoping it might convince an uncooperative peasant to help him. A metalworker provided a stick to help Idel walk. Pesach cut Idel's unruly, lice-ridden hair.

People too weak to crawl through the tunnel would be hidden in an attic. The hope was that after the escape, the Nazis would abandon the camp, thinking it empty, which would allow those remaining to make their way to freedom. Everyone received a number in the line. Idel and Pesach were put at the end so they wouldn't slow others down.

Thursday night, September 26, 1943, was dark and moonless. The wind was fierce and the rain steady. The escape was set to begin at nine p.m., when the guards were usually drunk. After waiting his turn for what seemed like hours, Idel was finally in the tunnel, pressing his arms and knees down, propelling himself forward on his belly. When he emerged at last from the tunnel, people were running, dodging machine-gun fire. Had the guards discovered their plan? Idel had no idea that the guards were shooting because they had seen the light from the tunnel but had mistaken it for the lamps of partisans who had come to free the Jews. He crouched on the ground until the shooting stopped.

Idel and Pesach walked in the relentless rain. They had eight hours until daylight, when the Germans would discover the breakout. The recent plowing had softened the earth, so it was slow going. Idel's metal stick kept sinking into the ground; he eventually threw it away. As he walked, the old wounds on his toes reopened. The two boys arrived at the river that had thwarted Idel in December, but he had no trouble crossing this time.

By daylight the two were too exhausted and wet to continue. Blood was seeping out of Idel's shoes. They crawled under a thick bush near an open field where shepherds were tending their sheep. It was risky to be so close to strangers, but they had no choice.

When night fell, Idel knocked on a peasant's door. They had to get something to eat. Idel clutched his pistol holder, but there was no need for his pretend weapon. The farmer willingly gave them bread and milk and informed them that the Germans were out searching the area. They gulped down the milk but only nibbled the bread, stuffing it in their pockets. It might be their last food for days.

When they finally reached Bobrowski's hut, all that remained was charred wood. They walked on for five more nights, uncertain if they were even going in the right direction. There was hardened blood on Idel's torn shoes. They drank from puddles.

Idel's cousin Berl Kagan, 1940

On the eighth day, they came upon people with a cart and horses. They hid and listened. Yiddish! The people were speaking Yiddish. They were Jews. Idel recognized someone he knew. They came out of hiding. These Jews were with the Bielskis and led Idel and Pesach to their encampment. Idel couldn't believe what he saw there — people were talking and laughing, as if life were normal. There were men on horseback with machine guns over their shoulders. How wonderful, yet strange, he thought, to see so many Jews here, seemingly unafraid. Idel knew there was no guaranteed safety in the forest. But among his people, he might survive until the Germans were defeated.

Pesach learned that his brother had been killed fighting as a partisan. Idel was lucky — he found his cousin Berl.

The morning after the escape, the Germans and local collaborators combed the woods, looking for Jews. More than one hundred seventy

Idel Kagan (second from left) with three cousins who survived the war: Rachel Konigsberg (Gurevitz), Dov (Berl) Kagan, and Leizer Sadan, 1990

Jews reached partisan encampments. The rest were found and killed. The Germans abandoned the labor camp, and the ten people still in hiding found their way to the Bielskis.

After the war, Idel learned that the Germans had discovered that Bobrowski and his wife had helped the Jews, so the Germans burned down their hut with them inside. The Bobrowskis' daughter and son were sent off to a labor camp. The daughter survived the war. Idel's uncle Notke died in Novogrudok a month after liberation in August 1944. His cousin Berl settled in Israel in 1948. Idel "Jack" Kagan emigrated to London, where he married and raised a family.

In 2007, the Museum of Jewish Resistance was established in the building where the digging started, and the entrance to the tunnel was discovered.

CONCENTRATION CAMPS

The first concentration camps in Germany were established soon after Hitler's appointment as chancellor in January 1933. Thousands of people, defined as "enemies" of the Reich, were imprisoned in these camps without any regard to their legal rights. Along with a network of subcamps, they served as holding centers for forced laborers working on SS projects. As the need arose, prisoners constructed new buildings for the camps and produced goods for the German war effort. The third function of a concentration camp was to serve as a killing site. Historians estimate that there were at least twenty thousand camps imprisoning Jews and other innocent civilians.

The largest concentration camp of all was Auschwitz-Birkenau, outside Óswieçim, in German-occupied Poland. Human transports rolled into Auschwitz-Birkenau day and night. Most new arrivals were sent immediately to the gas chambers. Those who were "selected" to continue living for the time being slept on bunks — more like shelves — in wooden barracks originally designed as horse stables. They subsisted on a diet of bread filled with sawdust, and soup that smelled like a sick animal.

Prisoners' toilets, Auschwitz-Birkenau, Poland, 1941

Background image:
The gates to the main camp at
Auschwitz bear the motto *"Arbeit
macht frei"* ("Work will make you free")

By 1944, Auschwitz-Birkenau had four gas chambers in operation, capable
of killing up to eight thousand people at a time, though this rarely happened. The
crematoriums could burn just over four thousand corpses in a twenty-four-hour
period. On the rare days when there were more than four thousand bodies to be
burned, the SS forced the Jewish *Sonderkommandos* to burn the overflow on open-
air "ovens" constructed on rail tracks.

Recently arrived Hungarian-Jewish women at Auschwitz-Birkenau, May 27, 1944

A Secret Celebration

Though trapped in the Lodz ghetto in Poland, twenty-six-year-old Israel Cohen defied his enemy by keeping his religion alive. The Nazis controlled where and how he lived and for how long he lived. The Nazis had burned the synagogues, stolen Jewish ritual objects, destroyed holy books, and forbidden religious services, but they could not take away Cohen's cultural heritage or put an end to his spiritual life.

Israel Cohen

Away from prying eyes, Cohen observed the sacred daily Jewish rituals. When the holidays came, he always found a way to celebrate. During one Rosh Hashanah, the Jewish New Year, he gathered ten friends in his family's cramped one-room apartment for a *minyan* and held services. For the Passover seder, they lacked most of the ceremonial foods but hardly needed the traditional bitter herbs to remind them of their people's struggle in ancient Egypt; their lives now were bitter enough.

Cohen had put the *tefillin* he used in daily prayer into its soft velvet pouch when he was forcibly taken from the ghetto and shoved into a cattle car bound for an unknown destination. In the car, he and other Jews prayed together, while others mocked them for remaining devout and faithful in such horrendous times. But Cohen answered that because God was everywhere, including in that cattle car, they would continue beseeching Him for His help.

The train arrived at its destination, Auschwitz, and unloaded its human cargo. A Jewish *kapo* spotted Cohen's *tefillin* and seized it, warning Cohen that he could be shot for such a transgression. God, Cohen knew, had saved him.

At Auschwitz, Cohen faced a hunger more devastating than that in the ghetto. The food was atrocious and minimal. He didn't even have a spoon with which to eat his paltry portion of thin soup. During the first week, he ate off of a single plate with two or three other people at the same time. They pushed the food into their mouths with fingers or pieces of wood.

Jews wearing prayer shawls and *tefellin* pray in a Polish ghetto (Note that this photograph may have been staged.)

One day he observed an armed SS guard pacing back and forth before a huge pile of potatoes. When the guard turned his back, Cohen took the opportunity to shove five potatoes into his pockets. When a boy carrying a bowl of rice and milk and a spoon later passed him, Cohen offered the boy his five raw potatoes in exchange for the bowl of gruel. The boy readily agreed, and Cohen realized he had made a poor trade and insisted that the spoon be included. Reluctantly, the boy handed over the spoon.

The gruel was delicious. Cohen couldn't remember how long it had been since he had tasted rice and milk sweetened with sugar.

Several days later, there was an unexpected lineup. A lineup meant being frisked. If Israel was caught with the spoon on him, it could cost him his life. He tore open a seam in his clothing and quickly shoved the spoon inside. As his turn to be frisked grew nearer, his anxiety that the spoon would be discovered grew more acute. He finally determined that he should get rid of it and was about to drop it to the ground when he heard a metallic sound just a few feet away. The SS commander had heard it, too. Money. Someone in line, perhaps overcome with the same anxiety Cohen felt, had dropped a coin to the ground. The commander demanded to know whose coin it was, but no prisoner answered.

Cohen stared hard at the ground while the guard whipped those prisoners who had been standing nearest the coin. The distraction gave Cohen an opening. He retrieved the spoon from inside his clothing, wrapped it in his cap, and clutched the cap in his hand.

"Hands up!" The guard patted Israel's body up and down, but found nothing and never asked to examine the cap Cohen held in his hand.

God had saved him again.

Ten days later, Cohen and three thousand other Jews were moved from Auschwitz two more times, finally ending up in Kaufering IV, one of Dachau's eleven forced-labor camps. He volunteered to work as a mechanic in spite of knowing nothing about machinery. It was a lucky choice. He found himself filing various metal objects and, when no one was watching, took out his spoon and hammered its handle flat, then filed the edge until it was sharp enough for cutting. Using it as a knife, he could now more easily divide his measly daily portion of bread into pieces, eating a little at a time throughout the day to stave off hunger.

Kaufering IV labor camp, Hurlach, Germany

Months passed. Soon it would be Hanukkah, the eight-day commemoration of the rededication of the Holy Temple in Jerusalem and the victory of a small band of Jewish rebels over the Greeks in the second century BCE. In Hebrew, the holiday's name means "dedication." As with all the other Jewish holidays that had taken place under German occupation during the past four years, Cohen knew he would find a way to celebrate. Observant Jews imprisoned in ghettos and in transit, forced-labor, concentration, and death camps found ways to celebrate their holidays.

Late at night, Cohen and other prisoners talked about how as children they had celebrated Hanukkah with their families. Most wondrous was recalling a father's passion as he lit the menorah candles — one candle on the first night, then one additional candle each night after until eight were ablaze. They talked of how the flames of the menorah sparkled

Lighting candles on the seventh night of Hanukkah, Westerbork transit camp, the Netherlands

like diamonds and inspired sanctity. They remembered the great Jewish heroes who overthrew the Greeks so that all Jews might freely observe the Torah. Following their victory, the Maccabees had lit their own menorah. But they only had enough oil for it to burn one night; miraculously the oil lasted eight days.

In the camps it was impossible for them to stop work on the Sabbath. They would be killed if they did. They needed a menorah. Cohen offered his spoon. They needed candles. Someone gave a bit of margarine that he had saved from his daily rations to be the oil. They unraveled threads from their ragged uniforms and wove them into instant wicks. Within minutes, Cohen's spoon was lit and the prayers were said.

The American Army liberated Israel Cohen and the two dozen or so survivors of Kaufering IV on April 27, 1945, and took him to a nearby farmhouse. The German farmer, fearful of revenge by the Americans, agreed to take him in. Israel, who had not had a bath in four years, asked to wash before eating. He took off his lice-infested uniform and threw it on the ground. The spoon was in the jacket. Weak and sickly, and unsure whether he would live, he did not care about the spoon. And so it was lost. Many years later, Israel saw a photograph of his "Hanukkah lamp" in a magazine article about the labor camp.

Hanukkah card created by members of a Zionist youth group, Lodz ghetto, Poland

Cohen immigrated to Canada. He has remained an observant Jew and continues to teach Jewish children about their heritage. Every Hanukkah he lights the candles of a menorah he created. It consists of eight glasses, half filled with colored water. Olive oil rests on top of the water. Eight wicks are inserted in plastic floaters and lit.

The *Sonderkommando* Revolt

AUSCHWITZ-BIRKENAU, OCCUPIED POLAND

Estusia Wajcblum (left)

Hanka Wajcblum

When the Germans marched triumphantly into Warsaw in September 1939, Estusia Wajcblum's older sister, Sabina, and her fiancé, Mietek, begged her parents to leave with them for Sweden. Her mother refused. She had survived German occupation in the last war and was convinced that she would survive this occupation, too. Nineteen-year-old Estusia and her fourteen-year-old sister, Hanka, wanted to leave, too, but did not feel they could abandon their parents.

Estusia and Hanka, who had dreamed of immigrating to Palestine, deferred their dream, as hundreds of other young Zionists did then. Instead, they worked at soup kitchens and at shelters for children whose parents were deported. In 1941, they listened to two young Zionists tell of the mass murder of Vilna's five thousand Jews. When Estusia told her father what she had heard, he told her he didn't want to hear such propaganda and ordered her not to worry her mother with such talk.

In May 1943, the entire Wajcblum family was shipped off to Majdanek concentration camp. The parents were sent immediately to the gas chambers. Four months later, Estusia and Hanka were in a cattle car destined for Auschwitz. There began the endless routine of Estusia's daily life as number 48149.

Every morning she dragged herself in the dark to roll call, then breakfast. After drinking the disagreeable liquid the Germans called coffee and eating a slice of sawdust bread, she walked two miles in her wooden clogs to the Weichsel-Union-Metallwerke munitions factory. There she and eight other women sat hunched over a machine for twelve hours a day, six days a week, mak-

Women's roll call at Auschwitz-Birkenau, May 1, 1944

ing detonators for bombs. Every morning, the German civilian overseer, Paul von Ende, doled out gunpowder. Estusia had to dip a tiny spoon into the powder and fill a one-eighth-inch hole in a steel disk smaller than a checker. When she pressed down the machine, the powder became an explosive. Von Ende marched around making sure that no one stopped work for even a second.

Still, Estusia knew that her work life was better than the lives of most women inmates. The worst jobs were outdoors: demolishing old homes, digging ditches in the mud with your hands, or being a human mule, pulling carts filled with hundreds of pounds of sand or the corpses of women who died during the workday.

The dust from the gunpowder in the *Pulverraum* (powder room) was a health hazard. The Germans wanted to keep these women workers alive so they would not have to waste time training replacements. So the women received one extra glass of milk and two extra slices of bread each week. The extra rations did not stave off hunger. Estusia thought constantly about food, remembering the milky goat cheese from the Carpathian Mountains that her mama used to buy at the market and the chocolate-covered rum-ball treats bought by their housekeeper, Isabella. Prisoners traded recipes and memories of tastes and discussed what they would eat if they ever got out of the camp alive.

The eight workers in the *Pulverraum* were the only prisoners with access to explosives. Roza Robota, a member of the Jewish underground in the camp, had asked Estusia to smuggle out gunpowder for the *Sonderkommandos*, who were planning to blow up the crematoriums. Estusia agreed without hesitation. So did Regina Safirsztajn, Eugenia (Zenka) Frischler, Ala Gärtner, Rose Grunapfel, and Estusia's sister Hanka. All knew that if they were discovered, they would be killed.

The smuggling was tedious. When Estusia pressed the gunpowder into the machine, there was always a slight overflow that spilled onto the table. Workers were supposed to throw the overflow away, but instead she swept it up and swapped it for fresh powder in the next batch. She slipped the few grains of fresh gunpowder into a rag. At the end of the day, she tied the rag with string and stuffed it into a small tin with a false bottom. Some women smuggled the powder out in scarves they knotted over their heads. Sometimes the powder was passed to Hanka, who worked in another part of the factory. She met Ala in the toilet in the factory, took the little cloth bundles from her, and stuffed them inside her dress.

The danger was not over after work. The women never knew when they might be stopped and searched — perhaps leaving the factory or walking back to the barracks. If they were body searched, they quickly spilled the powder out of the tins and ground it underfoot. If there was

Roza Robota

Ala Gärtner before the war

146

Forced laborers line up for work, Auschwitz

no search, the women huddled together back in the barracks and congratulated themselves on the day's bounty. On a good day the women might smuggle out a total of two teaspoons.

Estusia passed the powder on to Roza Robota. Estusia did not tell her friends or her sister who her contact was. Nor did Robota tell her comrades who her contact was. Knowing names was dangerous. Under torture, one might reveal information.

When Filip Müller arrived at Auschwitz in April 1942, as a strapping twenty-year-old from Sered, Slovakia, he was immediately assigned to

Background image:
Barbed-wire fencing and barracks, Auschwitz-Birkenau, January 1945

Crematorium ovens at
Auschwitz-Birkenau, Poland

be a *Sonderkommando*. There were now nine hundred men working twelve-hour shifts, day and night, in the gas chambers and crematoriums. New arrivals were assigned this work without being told what it would be. The previous June, when four hundred Greek men had accidentally learned what their work was to be, they had refused and were rushed off to the gas chambers themselves.

Müller saw his life as a living nightmare. He had to listen to the snap of whips and sticks attacking people who didn't move fast enough into the showers, which were really gas chambers. He had to witness the pained faces of those being led to their deaths. Through the thick doors of the gas chambers, he couldn't help but hear the desperate crying as the deadly Zyklon B filled the room. He knew the guards peered through peepholes into the gas chambers to make sure that everyone was dead

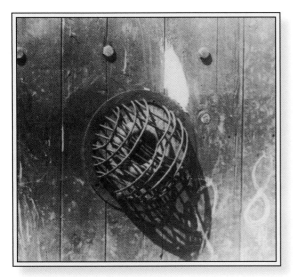

Peephole into the gas chamber
at Auschwitz-Birkenau

before opening the doors. Müller stoked the furnaces that burned the bodies of people who died in the camp. One night his father arrived among the dead. Filip stood with the other prisoners and chanted the *Kaddish*, the mourner's prayer for the dead.

He had seen people resist when they realized what the showers really were. One woman threw clothing over a guard's face, grabbed his pistol, shot him three times, then shot another guard. Other women attacked the guards with their bare hands.

*Sonderkommando*s were not immune from death. Three hundred were gassed on December 3, 1942. Two months later, two hundred men were selected to go to Lublin, Poland, for what the Germans called "special work." Proof that they had been murdered came in April, when Soviet prisoners of war arrived from Lublin wearing their clothing.

June 1944 marked a little more than two years that Filip Müller had been in Auschwitz. Only luck had kept him alive this long.

The transports bringing in the Jews had slowed. If there were no more Jews to murder, the Germans would no longer need the *Sonderkommando*s.

A woman prisoner who worked in the SS office had stolen a glimpse of a recent German newspaper and passed along the good news that the German army was retreating from Poland. The news convinced the *Sonderkommando*s that now was the time for an uprising. They doubted they would survive, but they could destroy some part of this death machine. They traded money found in the clothing of victims for a few revolvers and bullets from prisoners repairing weapons. They found three grenades on the bodies of eight Ukrainian guards who had been killed trying to escape.

They formulated their plan. There were only seven SS guards versus 140 *Sonderkommando*s in Crematoriums 4 and 5. There were 180 *Sonderkommando*s in Crematoriums 2 and 3 and twenty SS. The day shift of workers would kill and burn the bodies of the SS, seize their weapons, and put on their uniforms. When the SS night shift arrived, they would kill them, too. If this worked, they would have more than twenty SS uniforms and twenty weapons. *Sonderkommando*s who spoke German would put on the SS uniforms, wrapping yellow armbands on their right sleeves to distinguish themselves from the real SS so their comrades would not attack them during the uprising. A German-speaking prisoner in an SS uniform would ask a watchtower guard to come down while the prisoners went up to complete some necessary safety precautions. A gun with a silencer would greet the guard on his descent.

The uprising would be coordinated with work teams in other parts of the camp, who would kill their overseers and guards. The *Sonderkommandos* would burn mattresses and set the crematoriums ablaze. The gunpowder stolen by the women would set off explosions. Telephone cables would be cut. It was hoped that in the confusion and chaos, some prisoners would escape. Those who died would die with dignity.

The uprising was originally set for June, then postponed until August 15, and then postponed again. Toward the end of September, the SS asked for two hundred "volunteers" to work in another camp, promising better food and accommodations. Not one man volunteered, for everyone knew the "volunteers" would be murdered. That night the SS led two hundred *Sonderkommandos* to the gas chambers and personally burned their bodies.

On October 4, the SS selected three hundred *Sonderkommandos* to "clear rubble in a nearby town." Knowing they faced certain death, the *Sonderkommandos* readied for their uprising.

The leaders of Battle Group Auschwitz, an underground group of non-Jewish German, Polish, and political prisoners, were asked to join the uprising. The group refused, telling the *Sonderkommandos* to wait for better weather, to wait for the Soviet troops to move closer, to wait for partisans to rescue them. The *Sonderkommandos* were no longer willing to wait. Non-Jewish prisoners were not under imminent threat of death as Jews were.

On the night of October 6, the *Sonderkommandos* stuffed rags soaked in oil and wood alcohol between the rafters and roof of Crematorium 4. The next morning, when SS guards came to round up the three hundred

Crematorium 4, Auschwitz-Birkenau death camp, 1943

prisoners, they were pelted with stones. The guards shot at the inmates. Two guards got away and went for help. Suddenly smoke, then fire, engulfed the roof of Crematorium 4.

Müller heard the sirens wailing and the persistent rattling of machine guns. He fled into the crematorium room, looking for a hiding place. It was a long shot, but he didn't think the fire would reach inside the flue leading from the ovens to the chimney. He lifted the cast-iron cover, climbed in, and closed the cover. When night came, the shooting stopped. He crawled out, peered through a window into the yard of the crematorium, and saw guards everywhere. He retreated to his hiding place. The next morning, he heard the familiar voice of a Jewish *kapo*, a prisoner put in charge of other prisoners. Müller lifted the cast-iron cover and asked what was going on. The *kapo* told him to join the other prisoners in the yard. The uprising had failed. More than 450 *Sonderkommandos* were dead. Another two hundred had been rounded up.

The Gestapo found remnants of the homemade grenades and

realized the only possible sources for these explosives were the women workers in the *Pulverraum*. Regina and Estusia were tortured for two weeks. They denied knowing anything and were finally let go. Rose Grunapfel and Roza Robota were interrogated next. Neither broke her silence, and they were released, too. But a few days later, a Jewish

The gallows at Barracks 11, Auschwitz-Birkenau

informer told an SS guard that she had seen Robota talking to a male prisoner. Robota was interrogated and tortured again. A week later, Regina Safirsztajn, Ala Gärtner, and Estusia were taken away from their barracks.

A Jewish *kapo* sneaked Noach Zabludowicz, a friend of Robota's from her hometown, in to see her. The sight of his friend's battered, naked body on the concrete floor overwhelmed Zabludowicz with grief. Near death and still defiant, Robota assured him that no amount of torture would make her talk. Quoting Moses's admonition to Joshua, who was about to take over as leader of the ancient Hebrews, she told him, "Be strong and of good courage."

Three months later, at four o'clock in the afternoon on January 6, 1945, women prisoners were marched to a yard with a raised platform with two gallows. Draped behind the gallows was a long red cloth. Armed guards led Regina and Ala across the yard and up the stairs to the gallows. The sentence was read: "In the name of German law you are sentenced to death." Regina climbed the stool beneath the first noose. Ala climbed the second stool. The executioner dropped the nooses over their heads and around their necks and kicked away the stools.

Franz Hoessler, commandant of the women's camp in Auschwitz, mounted the platform. He threw his cape over his shoulders and ran his white-gloved hands over the women's swinging bodies. Then he spoke about Germany's power and warned that anyone plotting against Germany would suffer a similar fate. At ten p.m., Estusia Wajcblum and Roza Robota were hanged. As the noose was lowered over Robota's head, she called out *"Nekama!"* (Revenge!)

Before she died, Estusia had written a letter to her friend Marta Bindiger: "I know what is in store for me, but I go readily to the gallows. I only ask that you take care of my sister Hanka. Please don't leave her, so I may die easier." After Estusia's execution, Hanka's friends feared she would commit suicide by throwing herself against the electric fence and kept constant watch over her.

Thirteen days after the hanging, in brutally cold weather, the Germans learned that the Soviet army was approaching. Sixty thousand prisoners were marched through the snow for three days without food or water. Those who didn't walk fast enough were shot. Fifteen thousand people died before they reached the open rail cars that took them to another camp. Hanka had wanted to stay behind, but Marta Bindiger forced her to come on the march.

Marta, Hanka, Rose Grunapfel, and Filip Müller survived the death march and were liberated on May 2, 1945. Marta settled in Belgium. Hanka eventually settled in Ottawa, Ontario, Canada, where she raised a family and had a career as a social worker. Filip Müller settled in western Europe.

Marta Bindiger (left) and Hanka Wajcblum after liberation, Brussels, Belgium

DEATH CAMPS

Auschwitz was the name given to three different camps, all in the same area of occupied Poland. Auschwitz I was a prison camp. Auschwitz II, also known as Birkenau, was a forced-labor and death camp. Auschwitz III, also known as Buna-Monowitz, was a series of subcamps for forced labor. Belzec, Treblinka, and Sobibor were exclusively death camps. When the death camps opened, new prisoners did all the work involved in the mass murder of human beings — removing dead bodies from the freight trains, cleaning the boxcars, helping prisoners undress, cutting their hair, sorting and bundling valuables, and carting, burning, and burying the dead. Prisoners cut wood for heating and cooking and for the bonfires or ovens that burned the corpses. Young boys worked as servants to the SS, polishing shoes, cleaning uniforms, running errands, and cutting women's hair to be woven into yarn for slippers and socks for

After "selection," a woman and three children walk to their deaths in the gas chambers, Auschwitz-Birkenau, Poland

Interior of a gas chamber, main camp of
Auschwitz, 1945

Smoke rises from the burning of
corpses, Treblinka death camp,
Poland, August 2, 1943

soldiers. Women sorted luggage, cleaned SS living
quarters, cooked, washed and ironed laundry,
and tended vegetable and flower gardens.

At first the prisoner-workers were gassed
every few weeks in keeping with the Nazi policy of
leaving no witnesses. But constantly training new arrivals proved inefficient, so a
more permanent Jewish workforce was formed. Of course, violence and brutality
were so ingrained in the Nazi system that there was no guarantee that a so-called
permanent worker would not be killed on a whim.

Background image:
*Sonderkommando*s at Auschwitz burn corpses
when the number of bodies exceeds the
crematoriums' capacity, summer 1944

"Like Thunder in the Spring"

SOBIBOR DEATH CAMP, OCCUPIED POLAND

Leon Felhendler

Gustav Wagner

Background image:
Sign at Sobibor train station

The blasting, humid summer air had given way to slightly cooler days this early September 1943. It had been nine months since thirty-three-year-old Leon Felhendler had been deported from the ghetto in Zolkiewka, Poland, to Sobibor. Like most Jews in his hometown, he was unaware of the death camps until he arrived.

He was put to work sorting food and clothing brought by the unsuspecting Jews. It took him a few weeks to realize that the clothing had belonged to Jews who had been gassed. Felhendler had witnessed Nazi brutality in the ghetto. He had heard that people were arbitrarily punished and killed in the labor camps, but never in his life could he have imagined the mass murders of millions. Whenever the guards weren't looking, he hid gold that he found sewn into the hems and linings of coats. If he were ever lucky enough to escape, he would need it to buy food or shelter. And he would escape, or at least try.

Over the months, he studied the layout and organization of Sobibor. SS commander Gustav Wagner, who was particularly sadistic, supervised the daily life of the prisoners. Wagner killed Felhendler's friend Szaul Sztark because a goose he was in charge of got sick. When two prisoners did not carry out Wagner's instructions properly because they did not understand German, he beat them to death with a rifle. On Yom Kippur, the most sacred of Jewish holidays, Wagner took great pleasure in stuffing bread into the mouths of religious Jews who were fasting.

Thirty-two-year-old Kurt Frenzel, in charge of the selection process, was known for his loose whip. For his personal pleasure, thirty-one-year-old SS first sergeant Kurt Bolender set up boxing matches between prisoners, forcing them to fight almost to the death. When he supervised the railway platform workers, woe to the Jew who moved too slowly emptying the cattle cars of arriving prisoners. If Bolender's whip didn't get them, his dog did.

Kurt Frenzel

Camp guards were former prisoners of war from Latvia, Lithuania, and the Ukraine; they were offered freedom in exchange for working in the camp. Like their SS counterparts, some of these specially trained guards were vicious anti-Semites.

Escape seemed all but impossible, yet Felhendler thought about it day and night. There had been a number of attempts. One man had escaped in May 1942. In December, five Jewish women and two Ukrainian guards had run away, though both guards and one woman were captured and killed. In that same month, three prisoners had dug under the fences to freedom. In July fifteen prisoners attacked a guard and ran away. Eleven were caught and shot in front of everyone.

Kurt Bolender

Felhendler knew individual escapes were not the solution. The best hope was a mass action. And such an action had to be soon, before the winter snows came and made footprints easy to track. The transports had slowed. They used to come two or three times a day as Poland, Austria, Germany, Holland, and Czechoslovakia were emptied of Jews. It had been two months since the last one. What use would the Nazis have for any of them if there were no more Jews to murder?

Train depot, Sobibor

A new arrival had told Felhendler about the Warsaw Ghetto Uprising in April and of an uprising at the Treblinka death camp in August. Most likely he would die while escaping, but Felhendler preferred dying while attempting escape to letting the Nazis decide when he died. He had carefully formed his own underground, consisting of the foremen of the tailors, shoemakers, carpenters, and maintenance workers. He trusted these men completely. He had not invited any *kapos* into his circle because some of those inmates chosen by the Nazis to supervise the prisoners performed their own cruelties on their fellow Jews.

In secret meetings, Felhendler's group discussed possible actions. They knew the camp's geography, the routines, and the personalities and intelligence of the various SS men and guards, but they were not military men. As they analyzed each plan, they found major flaws.

On September 23, 1943, two thousand Jews and more than one hundred Soviet prisoners of war arrived from a labor camp in Minsk, Belorussian Soviet Socialist Republic (now Belarus). For the four-day, four-hundred-mile trip, they had been forced to stand and were never given water or food. Nevertheless, when the transport arrived, thirty-four-year-old Lieutenant Alexander Pechersky strode into Sobibor. His uniform was caked with mud and dirt, but the Russian Jew still wore it proudly after two years as a prisoner. His army cap still bore the imprint where the red star had once been.

Most of the Soviet POWs were sent immediately to the gas chambers. The lives of Pechersky and twenty or so other POWs were temporarily spared, and the men were put to work splitting trees into logs. Every day Kurt Frenzel ordered the prisoners to sing a German marching song as they went off to work. On his first day at work, Pechersky ordered the Soviet soldiers to sing a resistance song instead:

Alexander Pechersky

> *If war comes tomorrow,*
> *Tomorrow we march.*
> *If the evil forces strike,*
> *United as soon,*
> *All the Soviet people*
> *For their native land will arise.*

To Pechersky's ears, the singing was like "a clap of spring thunder."

The Ukrainian guards could have translated the lyrics for Frenzel but for some reason did not, and Frenzel remained ignorant of Pechersky's defiance.

News of his daring spread through the camp. Felhendler wondered if Pechersky might be the right person to plan and direct a mass action. Pechersky didn't speak Polish or Yiddish, and Felhendler didn't speak Russian. Solomon Leitman, a Jew from Warsaw, translated for the two men.

One evening Pechersky asked Felhendler about the smoke drifting over from Camp III, the fenced-in part of the camp where prisoners were not allowed. Was some part of that camp on fire? Felhendler

Background image:
Rail tracks at Sobibor
death camp

explained about the gas chambers. That night Pechersky dreamed that he tried to rescue his two-year-old daughter as she entered a gas chamber but fire swallowed her before he could reach her. The fire turned into SS men on horseback galloping after his wife. He tried to get to her, too, but was paralyzed. He woke up screaming, and then he wept.

On Pechersky's third day on work detail in the forest, a weakened, frail prisoner wasn't working fast enough to satisfy Frenzel. The Nazi whipped the man. Pechersky stopped working. Frenzel challenged him in broken Russian: "Russian soldier, you don't like the way I punish this fool? I give you exactly five minutes to split this stump. If you succeed, you get a pack of cigarettes. If you miss by as much as one second, you get twenty-five lashes."

The wood chips flew as Pechersky swung his ax, completing the job in four and a half minutes. Frenzel smiled and offered him a pack of cigarettes.

"Thanks, I don't smoke," Pechersky said, and turned his back. Frenzel stomped away but returned twenty minutes later with a loaf of bread and a slice of margarine. It had been a long time since Pechersky had eaten such luxurious food. He remembered the silky taste of margarine and the texture of fresh bread.

"Thank you," he said, "the rations we are getting fully satisfy me." He turned and went back to splitting wood.

Frenzel clutched his whip and left abruptly.

Pechersky became an instant hero in the camp. Felhendler was convinced that Pechersky was his man. The Russian agreed to help develop an escape plan. He asked for details on every aspect of camp life. What was the best way of leaving? Where were the land mines? How many guards were on duty and at what times? Where were rifles and ammunition stored? Was it possible to steal axes? What were the routines of the SS? What were their personalities? He asked for a map of the 145-acre camp.

Ukrainian guards manned the watchtowers. A water-filled ditch on the west side of the wire fence made escape that way impossible. But prisoners who had dug the holes for the land mines set around the perimeter of the camp confirmed that there were only signal flares behind the SS and Ukrainian barracks. Everyone agreed that their best

Barbed wire surrounded the entire camp complex. Camp I housed the workshops and prisoner barracks. Camp II was where the selections were made. Fenced off from the rest of the prisoners, the *Sonderkommandos* lived and worked in Camp III.

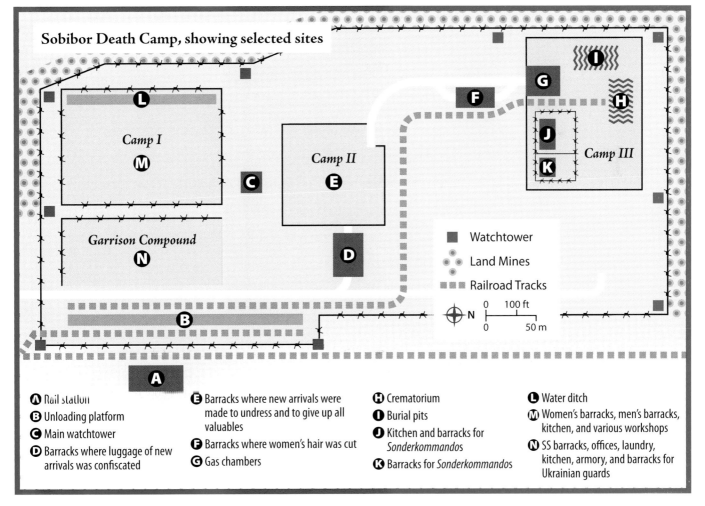

Sobibor Death Camp, showing selected sites

Camp I

L
M

Garrison Compound
N

Camp II
E

C

D

B

A

F

G
I
H

J
K

Camp III

■ Watchtower
● Land Mines
▪▪▪ Railroad Tracks

0   100 ft
0   50 m
⊕ N

A Rail station
B Unloading platform
C Main watchtower
D Barracks where luggage of new arrivals was confiscated

E Barracks where new arrivals were made to undress and to give up all valuables
F Barracks where women's hair was cut
G Gas chambers

H Crematorium
I Burial pits
J Kitchen and barracks for *Sonderkommandos*
K Barracks for *Sonderkommandos*

L Water ditch
M Women's barracks, men's barracks, kitchen, and various workshops
N SS barracks, offices, laundry, kitchen, armory, and barracks for Ukrainian guards

chance was to go out the main gate. An armed guard protected that gate, but there was only one fence, no ditch, and no mines.

Every three months, SS officers got three weeks off. On the average, there were no more than twenty-two SS in the camp at any one time. Pechersky wanted as many as possible killed. Three of the cruelest SS—First Sergeant Hubert Gomerski, Bolender, and Second Lieutenant Johann Klier—were on vacation. Wagner, the most intelligent and dangerous, was leaving in a few days. It was crucial that they act before these men returned.

Only Felhendler's trusted group of twenty and Pechersky's soldiers were let in on the escape plan. Telling the other six hundred prisoners was thought too dangerous. It would be hard enough to keep the secret with only their small group. Unfortunately, the *Sonderkommandos* could not be reached and informed of the escape. Pechersky hoped that once the uprising began, they would break out, too. Pechersky insisted at least one *kapo* be brought into the plan, for *kapos* were the only prisoners allowed to move freely about the camp. They could change people's work assignments without raising the suspicions of the guards. The first order of business, however, was to get rid of *Kapo* Berliner. Everyone believed he was an informer; if he even smelled the idea of an escape, he would tell the SS. He had to be killed quietly so the Germans would not suspect that he had been murdered. He was, and the SS never suspected foul play.

The breakout was planned to take place during working hours, when the guards would be scattered through Camps I and II. Watches were stolen from the warehouse so everyone could synchronize their actions. Phone, telegraph, and electrical lines in the camp would be cut. Prisoners working in the garage would disable all vehicles. The shop chiefs would easily lure the Germans, always greedy for new clothes, into their workshops for fittings. As the unsuspecting SS victim tried on a leather coat, a woolen jacket, or a new pair

SS and police who served at Sobibor, including a man believed to be Kurt Bolender (center)

of boots, a Soviet POW would wield his ax. Pechersky insisted that his soldiers do all the killings, because they were the only ones in the camp with any military experience.

At five o'clock, *Kapo* Pozyczki would blow the whistle for roll call. Soviet POWs, dressed in the uniforms of the dead SS officers, would march everyone toward the main gate, shouting orders in German. They had to hope that the Ukrainian guards in the watchtowers would not realize the SS men were imposters.

Pechersky stressed that once outside the camp, people would have to fend for themselves. There were no ghettos to return to, no Jews left outside to help them. It would be tough to survive. Most Poles would likely turn them in. Sympathetic Poles would fear for their lives if they helped. But if they could make it the mile or so through the forest and swamp to the Bug River, there they could join the partisans and fight the Germans.

It was a bold, risky plan. Any small slip could foil it. Like Felhendler, Pechersky was aware that the chances of success were slight. But if he died while killing some of the guards, he would do so knowing he had avenged the deaths of thousands of Jews murdered at Sobibor. And even if only ten or fifteen people made it to freedom, they could inform the world of Nazi barbarism.

October 14, 1943, brought sunshine and clear skies. It was the first day of the Jewish holiday Succoth, the Feast of Tabernacles. Escaping to freedom seemed a perfect way to honor God. Felhendler dug up money he had hidden. At 3:30 p.m., a fourteen-year-old boy brought a message to SS deputy commandant Johann Niemann, inviting him to the tailor's workshop to try on a new leather coat. As Niemann slipped his arms into the sleeves of the coat, out from their hiding places

Shlomo Szmajzner at age 16

stepped two Soviet soldiers with axes. Niemann's body was shoved under a table and hidden beneath a pile of clothes. Sand was spread over the blood on the floor.

As the killings continued on schedule, fifteen-year-old Shlomo Szmajzner, with tools and a stovepipe over his shoulder, walked to the Ukrainian barracks where rifles were stored. He told the guards there was trouble with a pipe. As maintenance foreman, Szmajzner often repaired the stoves, so there was no reason not to let him in.

The rifles were lined up neatly in racks, almost as if waiting for him. With pliers he cut the chains holding them together. He found bullets in a crate and stuffed them into his pockets. He tried to fit five rifles into the stovepipe but couldn't. The bolts were open. He tried to close the bolts but couldn't figure out how. Quick-witted as always, he wrapped a blanket around the rifles.

Through the window, he saw two boys working and called them over to give them the blanket. Knowing nothing of the planned escape, they panicked, cried, and refused until Szmajzner flashed a knife. He delivered the rifles to Pechersky and his men and kept one for himself.

By 4:45 p.m., the telephone wires were cut and the electricity in the camp turned off. The killings totaled eleven. The plan was going smoothly, except that Frenzel was still alive.

Then a guard walked into the garage unexpectedly and had to be killed. There was no time to move the body. Moments later two Ukrainian guards were killed. Their bodies were dragged to a place where the watchtower guards wouldn't spot them.

When Pechersky learned of these unplanned killings, he feared that their bodies might be discovered and ordered *Kapo* Pozyczki to blow the roll-call whistle. At the signal to line up, another *kapo,* ignorant of the breakout, shouted that it wasn't time for roll call. Pozyczki swiftly silenced him with a knife.

SS first sergeant Erich Bauer was bringing in a supply truck when he saw two prisoners fleeing from the body of a Ukrainian guard lying on the ground in a pool of blood. Bauer opened fire. At the sound of the shots, chaos broke out.

Pechersky and Felhendler shouted to their cohorts that it was time. They began firing their rifles, and from all parts of the yard, hundreds of prisoners came running toward the main gate and fence. The watchtower guards fired their weapons. Frenzel, hearing the machine guns, ran out of the canteen and started shooting. Pechersky took aim at him but missed.

Ladders were waiting by the fence. People pushed them up to climb

Participants in the Sobibor escape

over the barbed wire. Many got caught on the wire and were easily mowed down by the enemy. Pechersky crawled through an opening clipped in the wire and ran on into the forest. Behind him, he heard mines exploding and people shouting and groaning.

On the day of the uprising, there were close to 650 prisoners in the camp. Official SS documents and information provided by survivors conclude that more than 365 Jews tried to escape. Of these, only forty-seven survived the war. The Nazis and their collaborators tracked down and executed the rest. The Jewish prisoners who had not tried to escape were shot. Szmajzner and Pechersky joined partisan units and fought until the war ended. Felhendler survived the war in hiding but was murdered by anti-Semitic Poles after liberation.

Shortly after the uprising, the Germans destroyed all barracks, fences, and gas chambers on Sobibor's 145 acres, then planted trees to cover up any evidence that more than 250,000 Jews, 1,000 Poles, and two transports that included Soviet prisoners of war, had been murdered here.

Background image:
Site of the Sobibor gas chambers, where ashes of the murdered are buried, Poland, 1974

PART FIVE
PARTISAN WARFARE

This song was written with our blood, and not with lead;
it's not a song that summer birds sing overhead;
it was a people, among toppling barricades,
that sang this song of ours with pistols and grenades.

Never say there is only death for you.
Leaden skies may be concealing days of blue,
yet the hour that we have hungered for is near;
beneath our tread the earth shall tremble: "We are here!"

— From "The Partisan Song,"
words by Hirsch Glick, music by Dmitri Pokrass

HARASSING THE ENEMY

Partisans came from all walks of life. Teenagers, teachers, poets, artists, doctors, shoemakers, tailors, and homemakers escaped from the ghettos and camps and formed or joined guerilla fighting units. They operated in cities, towns, mountain villages, and forests, harassing the enemy and taking revenge. Some served as couriers, traveling illegally from city to city, from ghetto to ghetto, bringing secret documents, money, medical supplies, underground newspapers, forged identity papers, and ammunition. Geography played an important part in where partisan units developed. Isolated mountain villages in Slovakia, Greece, France, and Yugoslavia, and the forests and swamps of Belorussia, Lithuania, the Ukraine, and Poland provided cover for partisan groups. The flat terrain of Holland and Belgium made hiding and organizing much more difficult.

In the dark of night or in the brightness of day, in Paris, Lyon, Brussels, Berlin, Warsaw, Grenoble, Minsk, and other cities, partisans hunted and murdered Jewish and non-Jewish collaborators. They hid homemade grenades in their berets, pockets, and suitcases and placed them in soldiers' barracks and in restaurants where the SS dined.

Jewish partisans in a Polish forest
hideout, 1944

In the ghettos and camps, they planned uprisings they did not expect to win. When their uprisings failed, those who didn't die escaped to forests and swamps and villages high in the mountains. Outnumbered, outarmed, in the dark of night, they wrapped their feet in rags and forded rivers and traipsed through forests and over mountains to ambush the enemy.

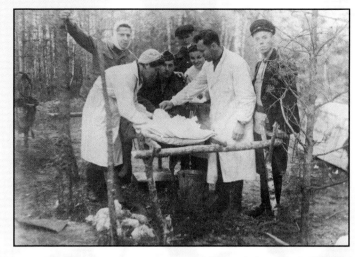

A wounded partisan is treated at a field hospital of the Shish detachment of the Molotov Brigade

With their bare hands, they pulled down telephone poles and ripped out telegraph wires. They planted homemade explosives under bridges and granaries and communication systems. They removed bolts from train rails and laid explosives under the tracks that had taken their loved ones to death. Then they hoped for the explosion of light and sound that marked their triumph.

A partisan triumph, USSR

Sabotage!
BERLIN, GERMANY

Marianne Prager-Joachim

Herbert Baum

Every morning, six days a week, twenty-one-year-old Marianne Prager-Joachim took the bus to work as a forced laborer planting trees at a farm outside Berlin. It was five years since she had helped her sister, Ilse, board one of the *Kindertransports* bound for London. In those five years, life as a Jew in Germany had grown ever more precarious. The one bright light in Marianne's life was her husband, Heinz, a half-Jew, who was as vehement an anti-Nazi as she was and had been part of the Jewish youth movement when he was young. He now worked ten hours a day in the Siemens munitions factory making fire-control equipment for U-boats. At night Marianne and Heinz held secret weekly meetings at their apartment with comrades to plan whatever actions they might take, however small, against the Nazi regime.

Heinz worked alongside hundreds of French and Belgian non-Jews who had been shipped to Berlin as forced labor. Non-Jewish workers at the factory were separated from the Jewish workers. But Heinz managed to make contact with Herbert Baum, whom he and Marianne had known from their earlier involvements in youth groups.

Baum had been politically active since he was thirteen. While his politics differed from theirs, the three were united in their hatred for Hitler. When Hitler first came to power, many Germans — Jews and non-Jews — dismissed him as a madman. But Baum believed that the madman meant every word he said.

Since then, Baum and his comrades had taken many actions against the Nazi regime. They had printed leaflets begging people to join their struggle against the Nazis. They wrote to four hundred German doctors, describing the real conditions being suffered by German soldiers at the front. Defying the curfew, they painted anti-Hitler slogans on fences and walls around Berlin. In the factory Baum was constantly encouraging Jewish workers to slow down production and to sabotage equipment.

Germany was now in its third year of war with the Soviet Union. The German people were discouraged. Too many fathers and sons and husbands had died in battle. Hitler had to rally people for another big military offensive against the Soviets by reinforcing the idea that the Soviets were evil. Nazi propaganda minister Joseph Goebbels created an exhibit, the Soviet Paradise, showing how millions of people would become "powerless, starving slaves" if Germany lost the war.

A blitz of newspaper publicity, newsreels, and radio broadcasts brought 250,000 Germans out to the opening on May 9, 1942. Baum and four other Jews took off their yellow stars and went to see what lies

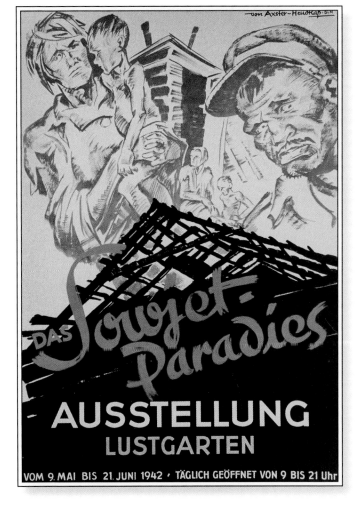

Propaganda poster advertising the Soviet Paradise exhibit, May 9, 1942

Crowds at the opening of the Soviet Paradise exhibit, Berlin, Germany, May 9, 1942

Goebbels had concocted. The exhibit was sheltered in a series of tents covering 9,000 square feet in one of Berlin's largest squares. A captured Soviet tank was parked outside the entrance. Greeting visitors as they stepped into the exhibit was a pile of fresh manure next to a replica of a "typical" Soviet hut of straw and mud. They walked slowly through the exhibit, reading lies, looking at anti-Semitic cartoons and staged exhibits, and viewing photographs of SS men posing as peasants and workers.

A worker's house from Minsk was disassembled and shipped to Germany to form part of the Soviet Paradise exhibit

There was a purported replica of a Soviet torture cell. The text claimed that nearly five thousand people had died in such cells. One photograph showed a confessional cell in which prisoners could only kneel. If they stood up, their heads would hit the low ceiling and trigger a spotlight and alarm. The cell had a small seat; if a prisoner sat down, he or she received an electric shock.

Text panels described forced labor camps "where millions died. The smallest offense is punished severely. Sick forced laborers are put on starvation rations to speed their deaths." In truth, the text described conditions in German labor camps.

The exhibit closed with a statement by Hitler to rally Germans to fight against the Russians: "We are now engaged in a conflict in which there can be no compromise. Either the German people will win and ensure the survival of the world and its culture, or it will perish, and all the peoples of the world will fall into the barbarism of the Soviet state that has reduced millions to powerless starving slaves." As always, Hitler blamed the Jews for everything: "If one looks for those responsible for these miserable conditions, one always finds Jews."

Not surprised but still horrified by the lies, Baum suggested setting the exhibit on fire. Marianne and Heinz knew that if they were caught, there would be harsh reprisals, not only against them but against innocent Jews. Still, perhaps by destroying this dangerous propaganda piece, they might awaken Germans to the truth. At the very least, the exhibit would close for a few days.

On Monday, May 18, at eight o'clock in the evening, Joachim Franke, Werner Steinbrink, and Herbert Baum carried briefcases containing homemade explosives into the first tent. Marianne circulated in the tent

Werner Steinbrink

as one of eight lookouts. The three men walked toward the fake Soviet village but found this exhibit closed. Joachim tossed his bomb into a nearby shack instead. Before Werner could get rid of his bomb, he saw smoke rising out of his briefcase. He ran out of the tent and threw the bomb into a sewer a few blocks away. Herbert's bomb shot forth flames and he fled the exhibit, too. All twelve left the exhibit ninety minutes after they had arrived.

Firefighters quickly quenched the flames from Joachim's bomb and cordoned off the burned area. The exhibit opened as usual the next day, attracting large crowds, and the Nazi-controlled newspapers never mentioned the incident.

A dragnet was organized to find the culprits. Four days later, eleven people, including Herbert Baum and his wife, were arrested. Marianne and Heinz avoided arrest until June 9. Another forty-eight people — some barely linked to any youth group — were also apprehended.

Under torture many were defiant. Heinz Rotholz stated, "I wish to add that I knew about the preparations of the sabotage action against the Soviet Paradise. Had the comrades not excluded me from the act because of my Jewish appearance, I would have taken part in the act." Lotte Rotholz said, "One must utilize every opportunity to fight against the present regime. My ties were and remain with Baum." Herbert Budzislawski stated that as a Jew he was compelled to fight, for it was the only way he knew how to "live in Germany as a human being."

Lotte Rotholz

Baum was tortured and beaten and his badly bruised body dragged around the Siemens factory, hoping his followers would crack upon seeing him. But they did not. On June 11, the police announced that Herbert Baum had hanged himself in his cell. His friends assumed he had died from torture.

Marianne wrote her parents from jail: "Think of the songs we all sang together, all is fine! Live well, my beloved parents!" Defiant to the end, as they were led to their deaths, Marianne and eight other women sang the "Internationale," the song that eventually became the official anthem of the Soviet Union. Marianne was two days shy of twenty-two when she was executed on August 8. Her death and her husband's were announced on large red placards all over Berlin. Over the next eighteen months, thirty-two members and supporters of Baum's group and other youth groups were murdered. Sixteen were twenty-three years old or younger.

As always, the Nazis retaliated against the families of those involved. Marianne's mother was shipped off to Auschwitz, her father to Theresienstadt. Two hundred fifty Jews who had nothing to do with the bombings were shot. Another 250 were murdered in Sachsenhausen concentration camp.

Today a monument to those executed stands at the western entrance of Berlin's Weissensee Jewish Cemetery.

Background image:
A veteran Maquis trains young fighters in the use of arms, the French Alps

PHANTOM PATRIOTS

Though Jews in France represented less than one percent of the country's population, they made up twenty percent of the Maquis, the French national resistance movement. French Zionists also formed the *Armeé Juive* (the Jewish Army): they attacked German forces and smuggled Jewish men across the Pyrenees into Spain, then on to Palestine. In Palestine, these men joined Jewish units of the British army and returned to Europe to fight the Germans.

The French Communist party created the *Main-d'Oeuvre Immigrée* (MOI), guerrilla units of immigrant workers ages sixteen to sixty. MOI groups operated as saboteurs, forgers, and couriers in Lyon, Marseilles, Toulouse, and Paris.

Jewish partisans before the liberation of Marseilles, France, 1944

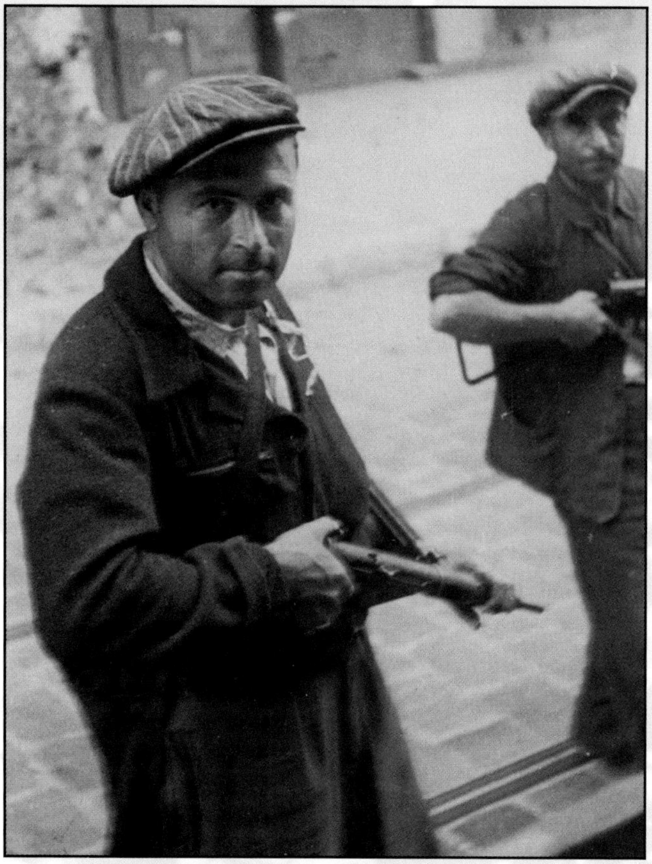

The MOI units were organized primarily by language or country of origin. In Paris there were four units — Jewish, Italian, Armenian, and Romanian, which included some Hungarians.

In March 1942, Abraham Lissner, a Polish Jew, joined the all-Jewish MOI unit in Paris.

Robert Gamzon, founder of the French-Jewish Scouts and commander in the Maquis

Members of the French-Jewish resistance group the *Armée Juive*

A meeting of Jewish Scouts in the forest, France

Long Live the Resistance!

PARIS, OCCUPIED FRANCE

Abraham Lissner

Abraham Lissner walked as casually as he could through the narrow streets of Paris, being careful not to draw attention to himself. Jews were not allowed out after eight p.m., but the Gestapo and the French police constantly patrolled the streets looking for them anyway. The French police could be as vicious as the Germans. Twenty-six days ago, they had willingly rounded up Jews in Paris, sending 13,152 by train to their deaths in Auschwitz. Gestapo agents were trained to recognize the slightest uneasy look or hostile movement of a person's face or body. If Lissner were stopped and questioned, his forged documents would probably pass examination, but his heavily accented French would immediately give him away. They would search him and find the small bomb in his jacket.

Lissner had been in hiding for the past year. He had ignored the first order for foreign-born Jews to register and escaped the two other roundups of foreign-born Jews for "resettlement in the East."

Jews being registered at the Pithiviers internment camp, August 1941

As a full-time partisan, he had no legal employment and no contact with anyone who was not part of the underground. Lissner had severed all relationships with friends and loved ones so as not to endanger their lives. He received a small stipend each month to cover his rent and food. Earlier that morning, as he did every morning, he had left his apartment along with all the other workers in the building so that the concierge would not suspect he was anything but a typical worker. He had been walking most of this hot August day except when he ducked into a café for coffee or to eat. He constantly changed where he ate so his face would not become familiar to waiters or regular customers. At the end of the day, he had returned to his living quarters, as all workers did, and waited until eleven p.m. to leave.

A woman courier in his unit had brought him the bomb that now weighed heavily in his pocket. Women often walked bombs from one end of Paris to the other. The Germans were least likely to suspect that women were transporting weapons.

His assignment for this night, August 11, 1942, was to place the bomb on the sidewalk outside of the window of a hotel restaurant on the rue Pierre 1er de Serbie, where the Germans had their headquarters. They dined in the hotel frequently and always asked for a table by the window so they could look out at people passing by. Lissner would have only a few seconds to place the bomb. If he lingered too long, a passerby might get suspicious and alert the enemy. The assignment, like all assignments, was dangerous, but he never hesitated to take one on. It was his responsibility, a commitment he had made to his people and to freedom.

He took the metro to the Iéna stop and met up with two other partisans. It was 10:45 p.m. The three men walked toward the restaurant.

Reaching the hotel, Lissner looked up and down the street. No one was visible. His heart was pounding as he placed the bomb on the sidewalk outside the restaurant window and set it to go off in ten minutes.

The three partisans walked at a leisurely pace back to the metro stop. Lissner's two comrades waited across the platform for a train going in the opposite direction. A German naval officer stood not too far from Lissner. He tried to relax and to control his body language. One wrong move or facial expression could give him away.

His comrades' train came quickly. He was still standing on the platform three minutes later when the explosion came. The station chief began shouting. The shrill sound of a police whistle pierced the night air. The naval officer glanced toward Lissner as if to ask him a question, but before he could, Lissner's train arrived. He hopped on it and was gone.

The Paris police and the Gestapo conducted a relentless dragnet and captured thirty-eight MOI partisans before December. In early January 1943, Lissner fled Paris. The authorities had identified him. It was too dangerous for him to stay in the city. He went north to Calais and blended in among the immigrant coal miners there.

According to Lissner's diary, in eighteen months, the forty men and women in his Paris unit killed more than three thousand Germans; bombed, burned, and destroyed nineteen hotels, thirteen warehouses, twenty-three military buses, and sixteen military groups; and derailed numerous trains transporting German soldiers and weapons.

As the partisans had more and more successes, the French people looked to them as heroes and liberators. The Nazis desperately needed to convince French citizens that these partisans were terrorists, not patriots. In September 1944, they plastered copies of a propaganda poster all over France. In bold letters, the Nazis posed the question: "Liberators?" Under the question were "mug shots" of ten captured resistance fighters in a group led by Missak Manouchian, an Armenian, and Marcel Rayman, a Polish Jew. Seven men were Jews. Only two were native-born. There were photographs of their various "terrorist" acts and statistics of their "criminal exploits." A show trial tried to discredit the partisans by insisting they were foreign terrorists. The resisters were executed on September 21, 1944.

Nazi propaganda poster portrays ten resisters as terrorists, France

When Lissner saw the poster, he could only praise his "dear unforgettable comrades." He wrote, "Your young lives were cut down by the enemy . . . an hour before victory, but your sacrifice was not in vain. Thousands of others are following your example, and are doing everything to complete as quickly as possible the great work you have begun."

Ironically, the propaganda poster became a memorial to the resisters. In French cities and towns, people handwrote messages on it: THEY DIED FOR FRANCE and LONG LIVE THE RESISTANCE!

THE OCCUPATION OF GREECE

Greece was dragged into World War II on October 28, 1940, when it was invaded by Germany's ally Italy. Five months later, the Italians had yet to conquer the Greeks. Disgusted with Italy's failure, the Germans intervened and devastated the Greek army in a single month. In the wake of this crushing defeat, more than thirty thousand Greeks fled to mountain villages and formed *andarte* (partisan) units. The victorious Germans divided Greece into three zones. German military units moved into Athens, central Macedonia, western Crete, Melos, Amorgos, and several of the larger Aegean islands. Thrace and eastern Macedonia were given to Germany's ally Bulgaria. For three years, the Dodecanese Islands and Evvia were under Italian control.

Macedonian partisans of the
Damyan Gruev detachment

The Occupation of Greece, 1941–1942

Bulgaria

Yugoslavia

Albania

MACEDONIA

THRACE

Turkey

Salonika

Greece

Ioannina

EPIRUS

THESSALY

LIMNOS

Ionian
Sea

Aegean
Sea

LESBOS

EVVIA

Steni

Chalkis

CHIOS

Turkey

IONIAN
ISLANDS

Athens

PELOPONNESE

CYCLADES
ISLANDS

AMORGOS

MELOS

Mediterranean Sea

DODECANESE
ISLANDS

German Occupation

Italian Occupation

Bulgarian Occupation

N

0   50 mi

0   50 km

CRETE

Invisible Warriors

EVVIA, OCCUPIED GREECE

A woman weeps during the deportation of the Jews of Ioannina, Greece, March 25, 1944

Sarika Yehoshua had seen the brutality of war firsthand tending the wounded. In the five months that the Greeks fought against the Italians, a steady stream of wounded Greek soldiers was carried across the bridge from the mainland to the makeshift hospital in Sarika's hometown of Chalkis, Evvia. Evvia is the second-largest island in Greece. Sarika was one of many Greek Jewish women serving as nurses.

Though she was only fourteen, the doctor had made her his assistant. She cleaned wounds, changed dirty bandages, and gave injections. She wrote letters to the soldiers' families so their loved ones would know that they were alive.

Then the Germans arrived in Chalkis. Clicking boots and shouts of "Jew! Jew!" echoed daily in the streets. Many Jews, including Sarika's married sister and husband, fled to the mountain villages controlled by the *andartes*.

News of the mass murders in eastern Europe had not yet reached the island, but the Jews in Chalkis were aware that the Germans had shipped off tens of thousands of Jews from the German- and Bulgarian-occupied zones of Greece to be "resettled" in Poland. A Greek resistance group, the National

Liberation Front (EAM), had issued a proclamation asking all Greeks to help their Jewish neighbors:

A new crime against our people is being planned by the conqueror. In Salonika, thousands of innocent women and children are threatened with executions, mass slaughter and concentration camps. This new crime is not directed only against the Jews, but against the Greek people, because the Greek Jews are part of our people, because their fate is connected with the fate of the entire Greek people.

The Germans turned Sarika's uncle's house into a dental clinic and residence and forced Sarika and her mother to move into a storage room on the ground floor. Sarika told her mother they had to leave Chalkis immediately. At first her mother resisted. Sarika sought help from an *andarte* who came regularly to town to recruit fighters. Sarika liked what the *andarte* said. He spoke of people helping each other, of being responsible to their community and country. He also stressed that women were as important as men and should therefore have the same rights as men. The *andartes* expected women to join the underground. To speak of such equality in Greece was revolutionary. Young Greek women from mountain villages were rarely educated beyond elementary school. They did not socialize with men until they were married. Their responsibilities centered on their families, not on the larger society.

Sarika and her mother were driven in a sidecar attached to a motorbike to Steni, a tiny mountain village three

Greek partisans Kimon Tsanthakis (left) and Into (Maccabi) Shimshi, a Greek Jew

hours away. The *andartes* provided them with forged identity papers: Sarika was now Maria; her mother, Zaphyra, was Zampho. They com-

Joyia Yaffe, disguised in a typical Greek costume, and her brother, Haim Raffaes, who was later captured and killed

pleted their new identities by donning the typical skirts, blouses, and head scarves worn by Greek women in villages. When the *andarte* decided that Steni wasn't safe enough, donkeys took them up steep, narrow dirt paths to another village three hours away, where they lived for two years. Sarika became the village teacher.

When Sarika was seventeen, the *andartes* recruited her to form an all-girl unit. Young women from the mountain villages would be invaluable. They knew the terrain and were practiced in navigating the impossibly narrow paths connecting villages. They knew where to hide in the forests. If the Germans saw sixteen- and seventeen-year-old girls walking about a village, they would never suspect they were partisans.

Sarika traipsed from one remote village to another, and from home to home, talking to people about community and the common good. Families took great pride in their brothers and fathers who were *andartes*, but Sarika knew that in spite of their patriotism, Greek parents would not easily take to the idea of their daughters being partisans. She had to be careful how she presented the idea to the parents and the girls. She did not say that there might be times when the girls would be in close contact with men. She said they would do women's work — nursing, laundry, and cooking. Even male *andartes* had traditional ideas of how women should behave.

Sarika formed a unit of thirteen girls. They called her *Kapetanissa* (meaning "female captain"). She wore a British soldier's boots. Her cap, jacket, and culottes were made from an American blanket.

Sarika's self-assurance masked the fact that she was learning how to be a fighter at the same time her troops were learning. She insisted that her unit get weapons, enabling them to join their male comrades in sabotage and surprise attacks. Her commander was initially hesitant and supplied her with only pistols, not rifles. Side by side, she and her recruits learned how to clean, load, and shoot their guns and how to throw a Molotov cocktail. At first the girls giggled just holding a weapon. Sarika spoke about courage. As equals to men, she explained, they must behave as such. As the months passed, she saw her recruits change and take command of themselves.

Kapetenissa Sarika Yehoshua

Andartes were scattered through many mountain villages but often joined together in actions. Every partisan answered to a local commander, and that commander answered to a superior in Athens.

Sarika's unit was frequently sent out in advance of an action to see if the coast was clear, then signal the men when it was safe. Once they were sent to torch an informer's house. The girls walked casually through the village until they reached his home. One girl went to the left of the house, another went to the right, and each threw a torch. The Germans never suspected that girls had burned the house.

Though most Greeks were fierce patriots, there were Nazi collaborators among them. The *andartes*, like partisans in every occupied country, showed no mercy to traitors. Sarika learned that a Greek man in the village where her cousin lived was an informer. The man had mistaken Sarika's cousin, who was a teacher, for Sarika. The Germans found and

187

Greek partisans are arrested by German soldiers

tortured her cousin. The informer was then given the "honor" of shooting the cousin in front of the whole village. Sarika asked her commander for permission to avenge her cousin's murder.

Sarika went to her cousin's village. She saw the informer walking about. She greeted him casually and asked about the Jewish teacher. The man proudly explained that he had gotten rid of her.

Sarika shot him on the spot, then turned and walked away, back to her unit, to continue the fight.

Sarika (Sara Fortis) lives in Israel today.

YOUNG WARRIORS

Background image:
Curfew notice, Poland

Partisan warfare against the Germans involved even the young. Long past curfew, children as young as eight slunk through dark alleys to paste anti-Nazi posters on walls. Children who worked outside the ghetto smuggled out printed appeals for joint actions of Jews and non-Jews tied around their waists. In eastern Europe, children acted as spies, gathering information, and as scouts, leading Jews out of the ghettos into the forests. Some children took up arms.

On May 21, 1942, after the killing units murdered two thousand Jews in Koretz, Poland, Misha Gildenman and his teenage son, Simcha, tried to organize a local resistance underground. But Koretz's Jews were too scared: many believed that if they cooperated with the Germans, their lives would be spared. Four months later, Gildenman and sixteen others fled to the forest, armed with only a butcher knife, one gun, and a few imitation pistols fashioned from bark. In a series of daring raids, they killed German soldiers and Ukrainian police and accumulated weapons. Uncle Misha's partisan unit grew as other Jews wandering about the Volhynia forest joined them, including twelve-year-old Mordechai Shlayan.

Simcha Gildenman, a Jewish partisan and son of Misha Gildenman

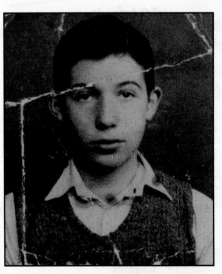

Partisan Dov Levin, age 14, Kaunas, Lithuania, ca. 1939–1941

The Violinist

Dyadya (Uncle) Misha Gildenman

By August 1943, Misha Gildenman was receiving daily reports of new towns and villages liberated by the Soviet army. Now that the war had turned against the Germans, some Ukrainians wanted to change sides. Keril, a friendly contact in the town of Ovruch, in the Ukraine, had sent word that police there wanted to surrender and give up their weapons. Gildenman knew the request could be a trap, but it had to be explored. He sent twelve-year-old Mordechai Shlayan, affectionately called Motele, to learn more about what was going on in the town. Gildenman had come across Motele sleeping in the forest and had taken the young boy into his unit. Motele had not been home when the Germans dragged his parents and his sister off to their deaths. He was the sole survivor of his family.

It was highly unlikely that the Germans would suspect that Motele was a partisan gathering intelligence. The twelve-year-old boy was small for his age and easily passed for Ukrainian with his blond hair, fair skin, and non-Jewish facial features. His assignment was to join the beggars in front of the church, play Ukrainian folk tunes on his violin, hang around the town, and report back anything slightly suspicious. In Motele's pocket was a forged document properly stamped and created by one of Misha's experts.

Motele maneuvered himself into the beggars' line of outstretched hands in front of Ovruch's main church. He took his violin out from its case and put a small saucer on the ground. He stretched his bow across the strings, turning the pegs until the violin was tuned. Then he sang a Ukrainian folk song that he had heard the beggars in his hometown sing many times. His crisp soprano voice stood out, and soon people gathered about him. He heard the click of coins in his saucer. One woman placed food in it.

The sound of hobnailed boots diverted attention away from Motele as a German officer and a nurse pushed aside the crowd and moved toward the young violinist. Motele did not see or hear the officer until he felt someone touch his shoulder. He looked up at a riding whip, immediately stiffened, then bowed. Would his forged papers in the name of Dimitri Rubina fool this man? But the officer never asked for his documents. Instead he ordered Motele to follow him.

Limousines and motorcycles flanked the entrance of the Soldiers' Home, a fine restaurant that had been taken over by the Germans to provide fun and the best food and wine to troops before they left for battle. Motele walked up a flight of stairs to a large dining room crowded with soldiers eating and drinking. Attractive young waitresses bustled about. The officer led him to an elderly pianist who was resting between sets. Motele did not hear their conversation.

"Do you read music?" the pianist asked Motele.

"Yes," he replied.

The pianist placed sheet music on a stand before Motele. It was a minuet by Ignacy Paderewski, a famous Polish composer.

Though Motele had never played this piece before, his performance brought much applause. The German officer offered him a job playing for two hours at lunchtime and from seven to eleven in the evening. His salary would be two Marks per day, plus lunch and dinner.

Looking for a way out, Motele explained that he was on his way to the city of Zhitomir to find his father, who was in a prisoner-of-war camp there. He said he was the sole provider for his mother and three younger siblings. The officer promised him that he would personally write the commanding officer in the Zhitomir POW camp and have his father transferred to Ovruch. Now Motele was trapped. He had no choice but to accept. It would be too suspicious if he refused. A good job like this was impossible for a boy to find. But what if the officer tried to find Motele's father and learned he was not a prisoner? Motele hoped the officer did not follow through.

The job proved the perfect front for gathering intelligence. In his free time Motele strolled about town, memorizing the names and layout of the streets, the location of government buildings, the number of troops permanently stationed in Ovruch, and the number leaving for the front. He passed the information on to Keril, who contacted Gildenman.

One night, the German officer asked Motele to report to his headquarters the next morning. Motele feared he had discovered that he had lied about his father. But upon arriving at the headquarters, he was greeted by a tailor waiting to measure him for a new performance outfit: a German uniform and cap.

Motele had noticed a storeroom off the basement kitchen where he ate after every performance. The room was filled with empty wine cases and wooden crates. The outer wall was cracked. Could a bomb be wedged there? Keril relayed Motele's idea to Gildenman.

The next step was to meet with Popov, Gildenman's explosives expert. It was hard getting in and out of Ovruch. Ukrainian guards were posted at the town's entrance. Luckily it was harvest time. Peasants were constantly coming in and out, bringing vegetables to market. Keril hid Motele in a wagon under straw sheaves. After several meetings with Popov, Motele learned how to assemble a bomb. For several nights, after performing, Motele hid his violin in an empty crate and sneaked the explosives into the storeroom in his empty violin case the next day.

His escape route was carefully planned. During Motele's free time, Keril showed him the way to the town lake through the city's back alleys and an orchard. They walked or fished or swam, looking for a shallow part of the lake where Motele could walk across. Once they found that, he waited impatiently for the perfect opportunity to set off the bomb. Finally he learned that a division of high-ranking SS was unexpectedly being rerouted through Ovruch on its way to the eastern front. They were not going by rail because the partisans had been blowing up so many trains that it was too dangerous. They would stop overnight and celebrate at the Soldiers' Home, where they would be greeted by Motele's bomb.

After three o'clock in the afternoon, the young violinist watched the SS officers in their elegant uniforms alight from limousines and motorcycles. Their boots were polished to such a glossy shine, he was sure they could see their faces if they looked down. The troops strutted up the stairs, oblivious to the bowing and saluting by the Ukrainian guards at the entrance. There was no rest that night for Motele and

Background image:
The 14th Division of the SS just before being transferred to the front, the Ukraine

193

his accompanist. They were expected to provide continual music over the noise of clinking glasses and laughter. Sometimes officers came up to them and sang along with the music. One man ordered Motele to play a tango. Another demanded a waltz. The officers danced with one another in high spirits.

At eleven o'clock, the pianist finally got permission for them to stop. A German officer sat down at the piano, and the singing and dancing continued. Motele went downstairs to the kitchen and told the cook he was too exhausted to eat. He said good night and walked to the store-room. He ignited the bomb, grabbed his violin case, and ran down the corridor. At the exit, he held up his right arm, giving the Nazi salute, and shouted, *"Heil Hitler!"* (Hail Hitler!) to the guard.

The guard laughed. "Ach, you little Ukrainian swine!"

Motele hugged the walls of buildings as he ran along his escape route in the dark to the lake. Behind him came the shattering noise of the explosion. Then police whistles and sirens. Motele walked into the chilly lake. When he reached a place over his neck, he held his violin up over his head. On the other side of the lake, ten hands reached out to hoist him into a wagon. With lightning speed, the horses galloped into the woods. When Motele calmed down, he raised his fists to the sky and shouted, "This is for my parents and little Bashiale, my sister."

When he was fourteen, Motele was killed during a German bombing. After the Germans were routed from the Ukraine, Gildenman volunteered for the Soviet army and served as a captain in the engineer corps until the war's end. He carried Motele's violin with him all through the war and brought it to Israel when he settled there in the 1950s.

Motele's Violin

Violin of Mordechai (Motele or Motale) Shlain (or Shlayan) who belonged to the 'Diadia (or Dyadya) Misha' partisan unit in the Volhynia forests. Motele was twelve years old when he fled to the forests after witnessing the murder of his family. He became a fighter in the partisan unit, and his reponsibilities included playing the violin and tracking the movements of German units. Motele was killed in 1944 in a German shelling.

Yad Vashem Artifacts Collection. Gift of Yousef (Seffi) Hanegbi, Arad and Zahava Shanni, Rechovot, Israel

In 1996, Amnon Weinstein, a master violin maker in Israel, began searching for violins played by Jews in ghettos, concentration camps, and forests in order to restore them. So far, Weinstein has restored twenty-four violins. "These violins are the voices of those no longer here to tell their stories," he said. In 2000, Seffi Hanegbi, the grandson of Misha Gildenman, brought Motele's battered violin to Weinstein. Hanegbi agreed to donate the violin with the stipulation that it be played when restored. In September 2003, before an audience of thousands in Jerusalem, sixteen restored violins were played in a gala concert in the Old City in Jerusalem. Teenager David Strongin played Motele's violin, which is now housed at Yad Vashem.

A film, *Amnon's Journey*, has been made about Weinstein's "violins of hope," and a traveling exhibit of some of these violins has been seen in Europe and in the United States.

I am a Jew and will be a Jew forever.
Even if I should die from hunger,
never will I submit.
I will always fight for my people,
on my honor.
I will never be ashamed of them,
I give my word.

I am proud of my people,
how dignified they are.
Even though I am suppressed,
I will always come back to life.

— Franta Bass, Theresienstadt ghetto, German-occupied Czechoslovakia,
age eleven, ca. 1942–1944

ACKNOWLEDGMENTS

So many people generously shared their knowledge and experience, never losing patience with my innumerable questions, but I am especially grateful to Israel Cohen, Ernest (Ernst) Fontheim, and Jack (Idel) Kagan, who let me into their lives and helped me tell their stories as accurately as possible.

I greatly appreciate the help of: filmmaker Myriam Abramowicz; Orna Alroy of the American Friends of the Ghetto Fighters' House; John Cox, associate professor of history, Center for Holocaust, Genocidal, and Human Rights Studies, University of North Carolina; Steve Bowman, professor of Judaic studies at the University of Cincinnati; Eric Brothers; Dr. Sheldon Brown; Barbara Cohen, spiritual leader of Congregation Ahavath Sholom, Great Barrington, Massachusetts; Anne Griffin, professor of political science at Cooper Union, New York; Bonnie Gurewitsch, archivist/curator at the Museum of Jewish Heritage — A Living Memorial to the Holocaust; Roman Kent, president of the Jewish Foundation for the Righteous and chair of the American Gathering of Jewish Holocaust Survivors; Michael Matsas; Daisy Rosenblum; Robert Rosenblum; Robert Rozett, director of Yad Vashem Libraries, Yad Vashem; Jules Schlevis; Rabbi Burt Schuman; Rabbi Avi Shafran; Siegmar Silber; Hermann Simon, director of the Neue Synagogue Berlin–Centrum Judaicum Foundation; Amnon Weinstein; Judith Whitlau at the Hollandsche Schouwburg Jewish Historical Museum in Amsterdam; Eleanor Yadin, librarian in the Dorot Jewish division of the New York Public Library; and Carol Briggs, director of the Roe Jan Community Library, who secured valuable books that were not readily available in my community.

I spent four glorious days at the Research and Documentation Center of the Ghetto Fighters' House Kibbutz in Israel, where Michal Gans; translator

Deborah (Schwartz) Jacobs; archivist Yossi Shavit; and Zvi Oren, director of the photo archives, shared their vast knowledge and led me to resources I would not have found myself.

The United States Holocaust Memorial Museum's outstanding staff was tireless in providing information and direction: Michlean Amir, reference archivist; Peter Black, chief historian; Nancy Hartman, photo archivist; Geoffrey Megargee, applied research scholar, Center for Advanced Holocaust Studies; Vincent Slatt, reference librarian, and Caroline Waddell, photo reference coordinator. Guides Ann Wiernicka and Ewa Wegrzyn in Poland and Michael Weiser in Israel enriched my understanding of their countries.

Michael Berenbaum, professor of Jewish Studies at the American Jewish University in Los Angeles, California, and former project director for the creation of the U.S. Holocaust Memorial Museum, critiqued the manuscript for accuracy and balance. Students of Elmsford High School in Elmsford, New York, and of the Mary Ellen Henderson Middle School in Falls Church, Virginia, were eager and helpful first critics. Joan Verniero and Sharon Harrison offered support and helpful criticism when the book was in embryonic form.

Copyeditors Hannah Mahoney and Renée Cafiero and proofreaders Martha Dwyer and Maggie Deslaurier cleaned up my act. As always, Candlewick's creative director, Chris Paul, along with graphic designer Rachel Smith, gave this manuscript visual dignity and elegance. My editor, Mary Lee Donovan, nurtured the book and its author with her usual intelligence, skill, and commitment. Liz Zembruski, assistant editor, meticulously organized the photographic sources, permissions, and credits.

My deepest gratitude is to my husband, Bob Rosegarten; it is no exaggeration to say that he lived and breathed this book — its people and events — with infinite patience, love, and humor.

PRONUNCIATION GUIDE

Prepared by Deborah (Schwartz) Jacobs, translator, Ghetto Fighters' House Kibbutz

Abraham Sutzkever, AV-ra-HOM soots-KE-ver

Adam Czerniakow, CHURN-ya-kov

Asael Bielski, a-sa-EL BYEL-skee

Chelmno, KHELM-no

Estusia Wajcblum, es-TOO-sha VAYTS-bloom

Feigele Peltel, FEY-gl PEL-tl

Friedl Dicker-Brandeis,
   FREE-dul DIK-ur BRAN-dice

Frumke Plotnicka, FROOM-ka plot-NITZ-ka

Hanka Wajcblum, KHON-ka VAYTS-bloom

Henryka Lazowertówna,
   hen-RI-ka LA-zo-ver-TUV-nuh

Josef Glazman, YO-sef GLOZ-man

Michal Mechlis, MEE-khau MEKH-lis

Mordechai Anielewicz,
   MOR-du-khai an-ye-LE-vich

Motele, MUT-te-le

Nachum Grzybacz, NA-khoom GSHEE-boch

Noach Zabludowicz, NO-okh zo-bloo-DO-vich

Novogrudok, no-vo-GROO-dok

Oświęcim, os-VYEN-chim

Pesach Abramowitz, PE-sokh a-bra-MO-vits

Ruzka Korczak, ROOZH-kuh KOR-chok

Terezín, TE-re-zin

Theresienstadt, ter-REZ-yen-shtot

Tuvia Bielski, TOOV-ya BYEL-skee

Umschlagplatz, OOM-shlog-plots

Yechiel, e-KHEEL

Yitzhak Zuckerman,
   yitz-KHOK TSOO-kur-man

Zacharia Artstein, ze-KHAR-ya ART-shtayn

Zdeněk Weinberger, ZDE-nek WINE-ber-ger

Zusya (Zus) Bielski,
   ZOOS-yah (ZOOS) BYEL-skee

199

IMPORTANT DATES

1933

January 30 Hitler is appointed chancellor of Germany.

February 2 Political demonstrations are banned in Germany.

February 27–28 After the Reichstag — the parliament building — is set afire, Hitler institutes a wave of arrests and terror throughout Germany. It is generally believed the Nazis themselves were responsible for the arson.

March 20 The first concentration camp is opened, at Dachau, near Munich. By the end of the year, there are fifty such camps in Germany to incarcerate political prisoners.

April 1 Hitler orders a one-day boycott of Jewish businesses.

April 7 The first of many anti-Jewish laws orders non-Aryan civil servants and public-school teachers be dismissed from their jobs.

April 26 The Gestapo, the German secret police, is established.

May 10 Jewish books and books by authors unsympathetic to the Nazis are removed from university bookstores and libraries and burned in bonfires.

July 14 The Nazi party is made Germany's only legal political party.

September 17 The Reich Representation of German Jews is established to represent the Jewish community before the Nazi regime government.

September 22 German Jews are banned from professions in journalism, art, literature, music, broadcasting, theater, and farming.

1934

January 1 Nazis remove Jewish holidays from the German calendar.

January 2 Laws are passed to sterilize the "unfit" — people with mental and physical disabilities.

August 2 Germany's president, Paul von Hindenburg, dies, and Hitler becomes president as well as chancellor. He rules unopposed as *Führer* for the next ten years and nine months.

1935–1938

The Nazis pass the Nuremberg Laws, a series of anti-Semitic rules and regulations that cripple the civil rights and social, professional, and economic lives of German Jews. Among the many laws are those that deprive Jews of citizenship, ban them from serving in the military, forbid them to socialize or marry out of their religion, and expel them from German public schools and universities.

1936

March 7 German troops occupy the Rhineland.

October 25 Hitler and Mussolini form the Rome-Berlin Axis, a treaty of friendship between the two nations, which later included Japan.

1938

March 13 Hitler incorporates Austria into the Reich.

July 6–15 At an international conference in Évian, France, on the plight of Jewish refugees, none of the thirty-two participating nations agrees to take in large numbers of Jews.

September 29 Britain and France sign the Munich Agreement, which allows Hitler's annexation of the Sudetenland, in Czechoslovakia.

October 28 Germany expels 17,000 Polish Jews. Poland refuses to allow the 12,000 refugees with expired passports to re-enter the country.

November 7 In response to the expulsion, Herschel Grynszpan shoots Ernst vom Rath, a member of the German embassy staff. Vom Rath dies of his wounds on November 9.

November 9–11 In retaliation for the assassination of Ernst vom Rath, the Nazis incite pogroms against Jews in Germany and Austria. *Kristallnacht* (the Night of Broken Glass) is the first widespread use of massive force against the Jews by the Nazis.

December 1 The first *Kindertransport* leaves from Berlin.

1939

March 15 German troops occupy Czechoslovakia.

August 23 Germany and the Soviet Union sign the Ribbentrop-Molotov Pact, a nonaggression pact.

September 1–28 Germany and the Soviet Union invade and conquer Poland. Over two million Jews are now under German domination. Thousands flee to eastern Poland and the Soviet Union.

September 3 Great Britain and France declare war on Germany.

September 29 The Nazis and Soviets sign the Treaty of Frontier Regulation and Friendship, officially partitioning Poland.

September 29–November 23 Polish Jews are required to wear yellow badges with the Star of David.

October 5 Poland formally surrenders to Germany.

December Nazis begin using gassing vans to murder mental patients.

1940

April 9 Germany invades Denmark and Norway.

April 27 Auschwitz is established near the Polish town of Óswięçim.

May Germany conquers Holland and Belgium.

June Germany conquers France and Norway. Marshal Philippe Pétain forms a collaborationist government in France. The Soviet Union annexes the Baltic states and parts of Romania. Italy enters the war as Hitler's ally.

September 27 Japan joins Germany and Italy as an Axis power.

October 12 The Warsaw ghetto is established, then sealed on November 15.

October 28 Italy invades Greece.

November 22 Emmanuel Ringelblum begins work on the *Oyneg Shabes* archives.

1941

April Germany occupies Greece and Yugoslavia.

May 14 Deportations begin in Paris.

June 22 Hitler breaks his nonaggression pact with the Soviet Union and invades the Soviet Union and its territories. Romania and Italy also declare war on the Soviet Union.

July 3 Stalin orders partisan units to be established.

July 12 Great Britain and the Soviet Union sign a military treaty to defeat Hitler.

September 3 At Auschwitz, the Nazis carry out the first experimental gassing of prisoners with Zyklon B gas.

September 29–30 Mobile Killing Squad C (*Einsatzgruppen* C) shoots 33,771 Jews from Kiev at nearby Babi Yar ravine in the Ukraine region of German-occupied Soviet territory.

October 1 Mass deportation of German Jews to camps begins.

December 7 The Japanese attack Pearl Harbor; the United States declares war on the Axis powers the next day.

December 9 China declares war on Germany and Japan.

December 31 Abba Kovner calls for armed resistance.

1942

January 20 Plans for the "Final Solution of the Jewish Problem" are discussed at the Wannsee Conference.

February 15 Auschwitz-Birkenau begins to operate as an extermination camp.

March 17 The Germans open Belzec extermination camp. By April 15, a total of 80,000 Jews will have been gassed there.

May 7 Sobibor death camp is opened. By the end of 1943, at least 250,000 Jews will have been gassed there.

July 22–September 12 Roughly 265,000 Warsaw Jews are deported to Treblinka extermination camp.

December 30 By the end of the year, the entire Jewish populations of many eastern European towns have been murdered.

1943

January 18 The ZOB attacks during a Nazi roundup in Warsaw.

February 2 The Battle of Stalingrad, which began on August 23, 1943, ends.

April 19–May 16 The Warsaw Ghetto Uprising

July 25 Italian dictator Benito Mussolini resigns and is arrested.

August 2 Inmates in Treblinka revolt. One hundred of the 300 who escape survive.

September 3–8 Italy surrenders to the Allies.

October 1 The Danish resistance movement and ordinary civilians with the help of Danish fishermen rescue more than 7,200 Jews, rowing them to Sweden and safety.

October 13 Italy declares war on Germany.

October 14 Inmates in Sobibor attempt to escape.

1944

May 15 Germans begin mass deportation of Hungarian Jews. By the 9th of July, 454,551 are deported in 147 trains.

June 6 D-day: Allied troops land at Normandy, France.

June 29 The U.S. Department of War turns down requests to bomb the gas chambers and railways to Auschwitz-Birkenau.

August 23 The Allies liberate Paris.

October 7 The *Sonderkommandos* blow up Crematorium 4 at Auschwitz-Birkenau extermination camp.

1945

January Soviet troops liberate Warsaw and Auschwitz.

April 12 U.S. president Franklin Roosevelt dies. Vice President Harry Truman is sworn in as president.

April–May Jewish prisoners at Ohrdruf, Buchenwald, Bergen-Belsen, and Mauthausen are liberated.

April 28 Italian partisans execute Benito Mussolini.

April 30 Hitler and his wife commit suicide.

May 7 Germany surrenders.

May 8 V-E Day. The war in Europe officially ends.

August 6 The U.S. drops an atomic bomb on Hiroshima, Japan.

August 8 The Allies set up the International Military Tribunal to try German war criminals.

August 9 The U.S. drops an atomic bomb on Nagasaki, Japan.

September 2 Japan surrenders, ending the war on all fronts.

SOURCE NOTES

INTRODUCTION

p. xi: "The biggest resistance . . . was to have survived": Jewish Partisan Educational Foundation. http://jewishpartisans.org/t_print_bio.php?pagename=mini+bio+short+2&parnum=31.

PART ONE: THE REALIZATION

p. 1: "I am a Jew . . . back to life": Volavková, p. 57.

A Wrenching Decision

p. 12: "Quite by chance . . . be related": Brothers, "Profile."

PART TWO: SAVING THE FUTURE

p. 17: "While you have breath . . . all the rest": Kramer, p. 128.

No More Saras

p. 29: "People are being burned": Vromen, p. 96.

p. 35: "Did they seem a little Jewish? . . . we heard nothing": Sister Marie-Aurélie testimony, USHMM archives.

The Most Important Game

p. 41: "Where are you heading?" and "To the railroad reception center in town": Georges Loinger testimony, Survivors of the Shoah Visual History Foundation.

"You Do Not Know the Extent of My Courage"

p. 44: "You Do Not Know the Extent of My Courage": Latour, p. 164, translation by Doreen Rappaport.

p. 46: "I will betray tomorrow . . . I will betray tomorrow": Ibid.

p. 47: "had to disappear" and "The German occupation . . . escape to Switzerland": Stein.

A Shtetl in the Wilderness

p. 51: "I would rather save . . . ten Nazi soldiers": Duffy, p. 108.

p. 52: "Jews! Have mercy! . . . listen only to me": Tec, *Defiance*, p. 117.

p. 53: "Partisans . . . guns and surrender": Duffy, p. 178.

p. 53: "Catch the Jews!": Tec, *Defiance*, p. 119.

p. 59: "Broken people . . . more and more blood": Křižková, Koutouč, and Ornest, p. 29.

The Final Solution

p. 63: "They want me to kill the children, this I cannot do": Czerniakow, p. 70.

The Warsaw Ghetto Uprising

p. 74: "What happened exceeded . . . Jewish men in battle": Mordecai Anielewicz.

p. 77: "The number of men, women and children . . . blood will be avenged": Dor, p. 184.

p. 78 : "The Jewish quarter of Warsaw is no longer": Stroop.

"Scream the Truth at the World!"

p. 81: "Scream the Truth at the World!": Kassow, p. 8.

p. 82: "Over the walls . . . an ordinary trap of life": Engelking and Leociak, pp. 448–449.

p. 83: "The whole truth, no matter how bitter, had to be told" and "the world would read and know what the murderers had done": "'Let the World Read and Know': Witness to the Holocaust — The Oneg Shabbat Archive."

p. 84: "A teacher asks his pupil . . . the pupil answers" and "A Jew had all his worldly possessions . . . my things, too": Huberband, p. 114.

pp. 85–86: "At the time I am writing this . . . fulfilled our mission": Kermish, p. 66.

A Banner Raised

pp. 88–89: "The banner has been raised . . . racial, religious and nationalist strife": Křižková, Koutouč, and Ornest, p. 36.

p. 92: "SENSATION, SENSATION!! On the day of the visit . . . throughout the preceding day": Ibid., p. 126.

p. 93: "As soon as the audience . . . memories we have of that place": Ibid., p. 64.

"Resist to Our Last Breath"

p. 94: "Resist to Our Last Breath": Kovner, "Scrolls of Testimony."

pp. 95–96: "Let us not go like sheep to the slaughter . . . to our last breath": Ibid.

p. 100: "Jews! Defend yourselves with arms. . . . Death to the murderers!": Rich Cohen, pp. 89–90.

p. 101: "What will become of me?": Ibid., p. 97.

PART FOUR: IN THE CAMPS

p. 107: "During the cold nights . . . buried her children": Matsas, p. 37.

The Ambush

p. 117: "Make sure you can escape . . . gassed and burn.": Schreiber, p. 237.

p. 118: "Don't jump yet. The train is going too fast" and "I'm jumping now!": Ibid., p. 236.

p. 119: "Leave, leave!," "It's forbidden," and "The Germans will shoot us all": Ibid., p. 226.

The *Sonderkommando* Revolt

p 153: "I know what is in store . . . may die easier": Heilman, p. 138.

"Like Thunder in the Spring"

p. 159: "If war comes tomorrow . . . native land will arise": Rashke, p. 159.

p. 159: "a clap of spring thunder": Suhl, p. 15.

p. 160: "Russian soldier . . . twenty-five lashes," "Thanks, I don't smoke," and "Thank you, the rations . . . satisfy me": Ibid., p. 16.

PART FIVE: PARTISAN WARFARE

p. 167: "This song was written . . . 'We are here!'": Kramer, p. 144.

Sabotage!

p. 174: "I wish to add that I knew . . . taken part in the act," "One must utilize . . . remain with Baum," and "live in Germany as a human being": Suhl, p. 67.

p. 175: "Think of the songs . . . beloved parents!": Cox, p. 442.

Long Live the Resistance!

p. 181: "dear unforgettable comrades" and "Your young lives . . . great work you have begun": Suhl, p. 295.

Invisible Warriors

p 185: "A new crime against our people . . . entire Greek people": Matsas, pp. 127–128.

p. 196: "I am a Jew . . . back to life": Volavková, p. 57.

BIBLIOGRAPHY

Thousands of books, articles, and memoirs have been written about the Holocaust. Historians have studied court records, diaries, memoirs, newspapers, and documents and have interviewed Jews who survived the tragic events. Many professional historians are survivors who have dedicated their lives to documenting their experiences and the experiences of others during this horrific time. My book, and all Holocaust research, is indebted to their meticulous scholarship and their courage and commitment to sharing their painful experiences with all of us.

Museums, libraries, universities, historical organizations, and Jewish organizations have put on the Internet important information not available in books. Here I discovered memoirs of people mentioned in books, lists of survivors of concentration camps and uprisings, maps, photographs, and video interviews. I have compared these sources and consulted professional historians and people who lived these experiences to provide the most accurate information. I remain deeply grateful to the individuals who showed incredible patience in answering my innumerable questions and shared their knowledge and scholarship. As Holocaust researchers continue their work, new information is constantly being added to the Holocaust literature. Any quoted dialogue in this book comes directly from the people whose experiences I have described. Some quoted material has been shortened without changing the meaning.

It was difficult to decide how to spell the names of people and places. Many of the cities in eastern Europe now have different names and are parts of different countries; many even changed names during the years covered in this book. In most instances, I used the common English spellings. In translating material from eastern Europe, I used the Yiddish translations, as these documents were originally written in Yiddish.

Many of the books I read are out of print and found primarily in research libraries. However, for further research, all websites included in this bibliography are available with the click of a mouse. Books that are starred are available in many libraries.

Bibliography Overview

BOOKS

Ajzensztadt, Amnon. *Endurance: Chronicles of Jewish Resistance*. New York: Mosaic Press, 1987.

Arad, Yitzhak. *The Partisan: From the Valley of Death to Mount Zion*. New York: Holocaust Library, 1979.

Barkai, Meyer. *The Fighting Ghettos*. Philadelphia: Lippincott, 1962.

Bauer, Yehuda. *Flight and Rescue: Brichah*. New York: Random House, 1970.

———. *Rethinking the Holocaust*. New Haven: Yale University Press, 2001.

———. *They Chose Life: Jewish Resistance in the Holocaust*. New York: American Jewish Committee, 1973.

*Berenbaum, Michael. *A Promise to Remember: The Holocaust in the Words and Voices of Its Survivors*. Boston: Bulfinch Press, 2003.

*———. *Witness to the Holocaust: An Illustrated Documentary History of the Holocaust in the Words of Its Victims, Perpetrators, and Bystanders*. New York: HarperCollins, 1997.

*———. *The World Must Know: The History of the Holocaust As Told in the United States Holocaust Memorial Museum*. Boston: Little, Brown, 1993.

*Dawidowicz, Lucy S. *The War Against the Jews: 1933–1945*. New York: Holt, Rinehart and Winston, 1975.

*Gilbert, Martin. *Atlas of the Holocaust*. New York: William Morrow, 1993.

Grossman, Chaika. *The Underground Army: Fighters of the Bialystok Ghetto*. New York: Holocaust Library, 1987.

Gurewitsch, Brana, ed. *Mothers, Sisters, Resisters: Oral Histories of Women Who Survived the Holocaust*. Tuscaloosa: University of Alabama Press, 1998.

*Gutman, Israel, ed. *Encyclopedia of the Holocaust*. New York: Macmillan, 1990.

Hilberg, Raul. *The Destruction of the European Jews*. Rev. ed. New York: Holmes & Meier, 1985.

Kowalski, Isaac, ed. *Anthology on Armed Jewish Resistance, 1939–1945*. Volumes 1, 2, and 3. Brooklyn, NY: Jewish Combatants Publishers House, 1984–1986.

Krakowski, Shmuel. *The War of the Doomed: Jewish Armed Resistance in Poland, 1942–1944*. New York: Holmes & Meier, 1984.

*Mais, Yitzchak, ed. *Daring to Resist: Jewish Defiance in the Holocaust: Essays*. New York: Museum of Jewish Heritage, 2007.

Marrus, Michael R., ed. *Jewish Resistance to the Holocaust*. Vol. 7 of *The Nazi Holocaust*. Westport, CT: Meckler, 1989.

Smolar, Hersh. *The Minsk Ghetto: Soviet-Jewish Partisans Against the Nazis*. New York: Holocaust Library, 1989.

Steinberg, Lucien. *Not as a Lamb: The Jews Against Hitler*. Farnborough, England: Saxon House, 1974.

Tec, Nechama. *Resilience and Courage: Women, Men, and the Holocaust*. New Haven: Yale University Press, 2003.

*Wiesel, Elie. *Night*. Rev. ed. New York: Hill and Wang, 2006.

Yad Vashem. *Jewish Resistance During the Holocaust: Proceedings of the Conference on Manifestations of Jewish Resistance*. Jerusalem, April 7–11, 1968. Jerusalem: Yad Vashem, 1971.

———. *Rescue Attempts During the Holocaust: Proceedings of the Second Yad Vashem International Historical Conference*. Jerusalem, April 8–11, 1974. Jerusalem: Yad Vashem, 1977.

Yoran, Shalom. *The Defiant: A True Story*. New York: St. Martin's, 1996.

WEBSITES

The American Gathering of Jewish Holocaust Survivors & Their Descendants. http://amgathering.org.

Ghetto Fighters' House Museum. http://www.gfh.org.il/eng.

JewishGen. http://www.jewishgen.org.

Jewish Partisan Educational Foundation. http://www.jewishpartisans.org.

Jewish Women: A Comprehensive Historical Encyclopedia. Jewish Women's Archive. http://jwa.org/encyclopedia/toc/all.

Museum of Jewish Heritage. http://www.mjhnyc.org.

University of Southern California Shoah Foundation Institute for Visual History and Education. http://dornsife.usc.edu/vhi.

United States Holocaust Memorial Museum. http://www.ushmm.org/research/library/bibliography.

World Federation of Jewish Child Survivors of the Holocaust. Arnon, Chana. "Jews Rescued Jews During the Holocaust." http://www.wfjcsh.org/rescuers/Jewish_Rescuers_chana4V.htm.

Yad Vashem. http://www.yadvashem.org.

Bibliography by Chapter

PART ONE: THE REALIZATION

"I am a Jew and will be a Jew forever"

Volavková, Hana, ed. *I Never Saw Another Butterfly: Children's Drawings and Poems from Terezin Concentration Camp, 1942–1944*. Prague: Jewish Museum; New York: Schocken, 1993.

The Turning Point

Beate, Meyer, Hermann Simon, and Chana Schutz, eds. *Jews in Nazi Berlin: From Kristallnacht to Liberation*. Chicago: University of Chicago Press, 2009.

Gilbert, Martin. *Kristallnacht: Prelude to Destruction*. New York: HarperCollins, 2006.

Nachama, Andreas, Uwe Neumärker, and Hermann Simon, eds. *Fire! Anti-Jewish Terror on Kristallnacht in November 1938*. Berlin: Topography of Terror Foundation, 2008.

A Wrenching Decision

Brothers, Eric. "On the Anti-Fascist Resistance of German Jews." *Leo Baeck Institute Yearbook* 32 (1987): pp. 369–382.

———. "Profile of a German-Jewish Resistance Fighter: Marianne Prager-Joachim." *The Jewish Quarterly* 34:1 (1987): pp. 31–36.

Cox, John M. "Circles of Resistance: Intersections of Jewish, Leftist, and Youth Dissidence Under the Third Reich, 1933–1945 (Germany)." PhD dissertation, University of North Carolina at Chapel Hill, 2005. Published as *Circles of Resistance: Jewish, Leftist, and Youth Dissidence in Nazi Germany*. New York: Peter Lang, 2009.

*Fox, Anne L., and Eva Abraham-Podietz. *Ten Thousand Children: True Stories Told by Children Who Escaped the Holocaust on the Kindertransport*. West Orange, NJ: Behrman House, 1999.

Freier, Recha. *Let the Children Come: The Early History of Youth Aliyah*. London: Weidenfeld and Nicolson, 1961.

Hacker, Melissa. *My Knees Were Jumping: Remembering the Kindertransports*. New Video Group, 2003.

Harris, Mark Jonathan, and Deborah Oppenheimer. *Into the Arms of Strangers: Stories of the Kindertransport*. London: Bloomsbury, 2000.

Kadosh, Sandra Berliant. "Ideology vs. Reality: Youth Aliyah and the Rescue of Jewish Children During the Holocaust Era, 1933–45." PhD dissertation, Columbia University, 1995.

Kadosh, Sara. *Heroic Acts and Missed Opportunities: The Rescue of Youth Aliyah Groups from Europe During World War II*. Washington, D.C.: United States Holocaust Memorial Museum, 2004.

Kaplan, Marion A. *Between Dignity and Despair: Jewish Life in Nazi Germany.* New York: Oxford University Press, 1998.

Leverton, Bertha, and Shmuel Lowensohn, eds. *I Came Alone: The Stories of the Kindertransports.* Sussex, England: Book Guild, 1990.

Paucker, Arnold. *Jewish Resistance in Germany: The Facts and Problems.* Berlin: Gedenkstätte Deutscher Widerstand, 1994.

PART TWO: SAVING THE FUTURE

"While you have breath"

Kramer, Aaron, ed. *The Last Lullaby: Poetry from the Holocaust.* Syracuse, NY: Syracuse University Press, 1998.

Coffee and Tea

Arnon, Chana. "Jewish Resistance in Holland: Group Westerweel and Hachshara." *Judaism: A Journal of Jewish Life and Thought* 196 (fall 2000).

Flim, Burt-Jan. *Saving the Children: History of the Organized Effort to Rescue Jewish Children in the Netherlands, 1942–1945.* Bethesda, MD: CDL Press, 2005.

The Jews of Holland During the Shoah. Catalog accompanying the exhibit at Beit Lohamei Haghetaot (Ghetto Fighters' House Museum, Israel), October 21, 1996. Bethesda, MD: CDL Press, 2004.

Secret Courage: The Walter Suskind Story. Produced and directed by Tim Morse and Karen Morse. Morse Photography/M&M Films, 2005.

No More Saras

Amkraut, Brian. *Between Home and Homeland: Youth Aliyah from Nazi Germany.* Tuscaloosa: University of Alabama Press, 2006.

As If It Were Yesterday. Produced and directed by Myriam Abramowicz and Esther Hoffenberg. Belgium: Ping Pong Productions, 1979.

Hollandsche Schouwburg. http://www.hollandscheschouwburg.nl/en.

Jewish Historical Museum, Amsterdam. http://www.jhm.nl/culture-and-history.

Jospa, Yvonne. Interview with the author, April 26, 1990. Christian Rescuers Project, United States Holocaust Memorial Museum.

Michman, Dan, ed. *Belgium and the Holocaust: Jews, Belgians, Germans.* Jerusalem: Yad Vashem, 1998.

Sister Marie-Aurélie, Mother Superior of the Convent of the Sisters of the Very Holy Savior, Avenue Clemenceau, Brussels. Testimony, July 13, 1945. United States Holocaust Memorial Museum archives, RG-20.019, Acct. 1994.

*Vromen, Suzanne. *Hidden Children of the Holocaust: Belgian Nuns and Their Daring Rescue of Young Jews from the Nazis.* New York: Oxford University Press, 2003.

The Most Important Game

Adler, Jacques. *The Jews of Paris and the Final Solution.* New York: Oxford University Press, 1987.

Dwork, Deborah. *Children with a Star: Jewish Youth in Nazi Europe.* New Haven: Yale University Press, 1991.

Klarsfeld, Serge, ed. *French Children of the Holocaust: A Memorial.* New York: New York University Press, 1996.

Latour, Anny. *Jewish Resistance in France, 1940–1944.* New York: Holocaust Library, 1981.

Lazare, Lucien. *Rescue as Resistance: How Jewish Organizations Fought the Holocaust in France.* New York: Columbia University Press, 1996.

Loinger, Georges. Testimony, February 1996. Survivors of the Shoah Visual History Foundation. www.lemonde.fr/shoah-les-derniers-temoins-racontent/visuel/2005/09/13/georges-loinger-passeurs-d-enfants_672678_641295.html.

Poznanski, Renée. *Jews in France During World War II.* Hanover, NH: Brandeis University Press/University Press of New England, in association with the United States Holocaust Memorial Museum, 2001.

Zuccotti, Susan. *The Holocaust, the French, and the Jews.* New York: Basic Books, 1993.

"You Do Not Know the Extent of My Courage"

Jewish Historical Center. http://www.jewishinstitute.org.pl/.

Latour, Anny. *Jewish Resistance in France, 1940–1944.* New York: Holocaust Library, 1981.

Lefenfeld, Nancy. "Mila Racine and Marianne Cohn: Two Jews Who Rescued Jews in Nazi Europe." *Mishpocha!* Newsletter of the World Federation of Jewish Child Survivors of the Holocaust. Conshohocken, PA: summer 2003.

Stein, Helen Koenig. "France: Memoir of Helen Koenig Stein." *Mishpocha!* Newsletter of the World Federation of Jewish Child Survivors of the Holocaust. Conshohocken, PA: spring 2005.

A Shtetl in the Wilderness

Amarant, Shmuel. "The Partisans of Tuvia Bielski." Chapter in *Surviving the Holocaust with the Russian Jewish Partisans,* edited by Jack Kagan and Dov Cohen. London: Vallentine Mitchell, 1998.

Bielski, Tuvia. *Yehudei Ya'ar, Sefer Milchamot Hageta'ot.* Edited by Yitzchak Zuckerman Basuk. Hakibutz Hameuchad Publishing and Kibbutz Lohamei Haghetaot, 1954.

The Bielski Brothers: Jerusalem in the Woods. Written and directed by Dean Ward. The History Channel, 2006.

*Duffy, Peter. *The Bielski Brothers: The True Story of Three Men Who Defied the Nazis, Saved 1,200 Jews, and Built a Village in the Forest.* New York: HarperCollins, 2003.

Florida Holocaust Museum. "Courage and Compassion: The Legacy of the Bielski Brothers." http://www.courageandcompassionexhibit.com/about-the-florida-holocaust-museum.aspx.

Jewish Partisan Educational Foundation. http://www.jewishpartisans.org/pdfs/Tuvia_Bielski_Study_Guide.pdf.

*Levine, Allan Gerald. *Fugitives of the Forest: The Heroic Story of Jewish Resistance and Survival During the Second World War.* Toronto: Stoddart, 1998.

*Tec, Nechama. *Defiance: The Bielski Partisans.* New York: Oxford University Press, 1993.

The Tuvia and Lilka Bielski Family Foundation. http://www.bielskifoundation.org/.

PART THREE: IN THE GHETTOS

"Broken people"

Křižková, Marie Rút, Kurt Jiří Koutouč, and Zdeněk Ornest, eds. *We Are Children Just the Same: Vedem, the Secret Magazine by the Boys of Terezín.* Philadelphia: Jewish Publication Society, 1995.

The Final Solution

Czerniakow, Adam. *The Warsaw Diary of Adam Czerniakow: Prelude to Doom.* Edited by Raul Hilberg, Stanislaw Staron, and Josef Kermisz. Translated by Stanislaw Staron and the staff at Yad Vashem. Published by Ivan R. Dee in association with the USHMM, 1999.

The Warsaw Ghetto Uprising

Anielewicz, Mordecai. "The Last Letter from Ghetto Revolt Commander Mordecai Anielewicz, Warsaw." *Documents on the Holocaust, selected sources on the Destruction of the Jews in Germany and Austria, Poland and the Soviet Union.* Yad Vashem, Jerusalem, 1981. Document no. 145. www.yadvashem.org.

Chronicle of the Warsaw Ghetto Uprising According to Marek Edelman. Directed by Joland Dylewska. Warsaw, 1994.

Dor, Danny, Ilan Kfir, and Chava Biran. *Brave and Desperate: The Warsaw Ghetto Uprising.* Israel: Ghetto Fighters' House Museum, 2003.

Edelman, Marek. "The Ghetto Fights," in *The Warsaw Ghetto: The 45th Anniversary of the Uprising.* London: Interpress Publishers, 1990.

Engelking-Boni, Barbara, and Jacek Leociak. *The Warsaw Ghetto: A Guide to the Perished City.* New Haven: Yale University Press, 2009.

Glassman, Gary Scott. "The Couriers of the Jewish Underground in Poland During the Holocaust." PhD dissertation, California State University, 2001.

Gutman, Israel. *The Jews of Warsaw, 1939–1943: Ghetto, Underground, Revolt.* Bloomington: Indiana University Press, 1982.

Krall, Hanna. *Shielding the Flame: An Intimate Conversation with Dr. Marek Edelman, the Last Surviving Leader of the Warsaw Ghetto Uprising.* New York: Holt, 1986.

*Kurzman, Dan. *The Bravest Battle: The Twenty-eight Days of the Warsaw Ghetto Uprising.* New York: Putnam, 1976.

Mark, Ber. *Uprising in the Warsaw Ghetto.* New York: Schocken, 1975.

*Miedzyrzecki, Feigele Peltel. *On Both Sides of the Wall: Memoirs from the Warsaw Ghetto.* New York: Holocaust Library, 1979.

*Rotem, Simha. *Memoirs of a Warsaw Ghetto Fighter: The Past Within Me.* New Haven: Yale University Press, 1994.

Stroop, Jürgen. *The Stroop Report: The Jewish Quarter Is No More!* Translated from the German and annotated by Sybil Milton, with an introduction by Andrzej Wirth Stroop. New York: Pantheon, 1979.

*Zuckerman, Yitzhak. *A Surplus of Memory: Chronicle of the Warsaw Ghetto Uprising.* Berkeley: University of California Press, 1993.

"Scream the Truth at the World!"

The Emanuel Ringelblum Jewish Historical Institute. http://www.jewishinstitute.org.pl.

Engelking-Boni, Barbara, and Jacek Leociak. *The Warsaw Ghetto: A Guide to the Perished City.* New Haven: Yale University Press, 2009.

Huberband, Shimon. *Kiddush Hashem: Jewish Religious and Cultural Life in Poland During the Holocaust.* New York: Yeshiva University Press, 1987.

Jewish Historical Institute Kalendarium. http://jewishinstitute.org.pl/en/home.historical/l.html.

*Kassow, Samuel. *Who Will Write Our History? Emanuel Ringelblum, the Warsaw Ghetto, and the Oyneg Shabes Archive.* Bloomington: Indiana University Press, 2007.

Kermish, Joseph, ed. *To Live with Honor and Die with Honor: Selected Documents from the Warsaw Ghetto Underground Archives "O.S." ("Oneg Shabbath")*. Jerusalem: Yad Vashem, 1986.

"'Let the World Read and Know': Witness to the Holocaust — The Oneg Shabbat Archives," Yad Vashem website, http://www1.yadvashem.org/yv/en/exhibitions/ringelbum/intro.asp.

Ringelblum, Emmanuel. *Notes from the Warsaw Ghetto: The Journal of Emmanuel Ringelblum*. New York: McGraw-Hill, 1958.

A Banner Raised

*Ginz, Petr. *The Diary of Petr Ginz, 1941–1942*. New York: Atlantic Monthly Press, 2007.

Jewish Museum in Prague. http://www.jewishmuseum.cz.

*Křižková, Marie Rút, Kurt Jiří Koutouč, and Zdeněk Ornest, eds. *We Are Children Just the Same: Vedem, the Secret Magazine by the Boys of Terezín*. Philadelphia: Jewish Publication Society, 1995.

*Makarova, Elena. *Friedl Dicker-Brandeis, Vienna 1898–Auschwitz 1944: The Artist Who Inspired the Children's Drawings of Terezin*. Los Angeles: Tallfellow/Every Picture Press, in association with the Simon Wiesenthal Center/Museum of Tolerance, 2001.

Novitch, Miriam, Lucy S. Dawidowicz, and Tom L. Freudenheim. *Spiritual Resistance: Art from Concentration Camps, 1940–1945: A Selection of Drawings and Paintings from the Collection of Kibbutz Lohamei Haghetaot, Israel*. New York: Union of American Hebrew Congregations, 1981.

*Rubin, Susan Goldman. *Fireflies in the Dark: The Story of Friedl Dicker-Brandeis and the Children of Terezin*. New York: Holiday House, 2000.

Theresienstadt Martyrs Remembrance Association. http://www.bterezin.org.il.

Theresienstadt Memorial (Památník Theresienstadt). www.s.pamatnik-terezin.cz.

*Thomson, Ruth. *Terezín: Voices from the Holocaust*. Somerville, MA: Candlewick Press, 2011.

*Volavková, Hana, ed. *I Never Saw Another Butterfly: Children's Drawings and Poems from Terezin Concentration Camp, 1942–1944*. Prague: Jewish Museum; New York: Schocken, 1993.

"Resist to Our Last Breath"

*Bart, Michael, and Laurel Corona. *Until Our Last Breath: A Holocaust Story of Love and Partisan Resistance*. New York: St. Martin's, 2008.

*Cohen, Rich. *The Avengers. A Jewish War Story*. New York: Knopf, 2000.

Eckman, Lester Samuel, and Chaim Lazar. *The Jewish Resistance: The History of the Jewish Partisans in Lithuania and White Russia During the Nazi Occupation, 1940–1945*. New York: Shengold, 1977.

Harmatz, Joseph. *From the Wings: A Long Journey: 1940–1960*. Sussex, England: Book Guild, 1998.

Kovner, Abba. "A First Attempt to Tell." In *The Holocaust as Historical Experience: Essays and a Discussion*, edited by Yehuda Bauer. New York: Holmes & Meier, 1981.

———. *Scrolls of Testimony*. Philadelphia: Jewish Publication Society, 2001.

Kruk, Herman. *The Last Days of the Jerusalem of Lithuania: Chronicles from the Vilna Ghetto and Camps, 1939–1944*. New Haven: YIVO Institute for Jewish Research, 2002.

Levin, Dov. *Fighting Back: Lithuanian Jewry's Armed Resistance to the Nazis, 1941–1945*. New York: Holmes & Meier, 1985.

The Nizkor Project. http://www.nizkor.org.

Shames, Morton. "Memoirs of a Machine-Gunner." In *Anthology on Armed Jewish Resistance 1939–1945*, edited by Isaac Kowalski. New York: Jewish Combatants Publishers House, 1985.

Waletzky, Josh. *Partisans of Vilna. The Untold Story of Jewish Resistance During World War II*. Washington, D.C.: Ciesla Foundation, 1986.

PART FOUR: IN THE CAMPS

"During the cold nights"

Matsas, Michael. *The Illusion of Safety: The Story of the Greek Jews During the Second World War*. New York: Pella, 1997.

The Ambush

Griffin, Anne, and Jean-Marc Gourdon. "Resistance and Memory in Belgium, 1940–1945." The Cooper Union for the Advancement of Science and Art, 2005. Yeshiva University Museum, 2006–2007. Verzetsmuseum, Amsterdam, 2008.

"Simon Gronowski, Survivor XXth Convoy." http://users.telenet.be/holocaust.bmb/eng/Gronowski.htm.

Kles, Shlomo. "Resistance and Fighting in Belgium During the Holocaust." *Zion* 47:4 (1982): pp. 463–482.

Krochmal, Regine. "Regine Krochmal: Nurse, Jewish Resistance, Survivor 20th Convoy." http://users.telenet.be/holocaust.bmb/eng/Krochmal.htm.

*Schreiber, Marion. *The Twentieth Train: The True Story of the Ambush of the Death Train to Auschwitz*. New York: Grove Press, 2003.

Steinberg, Lucien. "Jewish Rescue Activities in Belgium and France." http://www1.yadvashem.org/yv/en/righteous/pdf/resources/lucien_steinberg.pdf.

Three Feet a Day

Ferencz, Benjamin B. *Less than Slaves: Jewish Forced Labor and the Quest for Compensation.* Bloomington: Indiana University Press, in association with the United States Holocaust Memorial Museum, 2002.

Kagan, Idel. "How I Survived." Navaredok Memorial Book. Translation of *Pinkas Navaredok*, edited by E. Yerushalmi. Tel Aviv, Israel, 1963. http://www.jewishgen.org/yizkor/Novogrudok/nov299.html.

Kagan, Jack, ed. *Novogrudok: The History of a Shtetl.* London: Vallentine Mitchell, 1998.

——— and Dov Cohen. *Surviving the Holocaust with the Russian Jewish Partisans.* London: Vallentine Mitchell, 1998.

Museum of Jewish Resistance in Novogrudok. http://jrmn.info/en.

Novogrudek: The History of a Jewish Shtetl. http://www.novogrudek.co.uk.

A Secret Celebration

Cohen, Israel. *Destined to Survive: Uplifting Stories from the Worst of Times.* Brooklyn, NY: Mesorah Publications, 2001.

The *Sonderkommando* Revolt

Bezwinska, Jadwiga, and Danuta Czech, eds. *Amidst a Nightmare of Crime: Manuscripts of the Prisoners in Crematorium Squads Found at Auschwitz.* New York: H. Fertig, 1992.

Cohen, Leon. *From Greece to Birkenau: The Crematoria Workers' Uprising.* Tel Aviv: Salonika Jewry Research Center, 1996.

Garliński, Józef. *Fighting Auschwitz: The Resistance Movement in the Concentration Camp.* London: Julian Friedmann, 1975.

Greif, Gideon. *We Wept Without Tears: Testimonies of the Jewish Sonderkommando from Auschwitz.* New Haven: Yale University Press, 2005.

*Gutman, Yisrael, and Michael Berenbaum, eds. *Anatomy of the Auschwitz Death Camp.* Bloomington: Indiana University Press, 1994.

*Heilman, Anna. *Never Far Away: The Auschwitz Chronicles of Anna Heilman.* Calgary: University of Calgary Press, 2001.

———. Transcript at SHOAH from the United States Holocaust Museum, from SHOAH Interviews. Auschwitz II Birkenau video copyright 1994–2007 by Morris Venezia, Morris Gesselman, and Dario Gabbio.

Kraus, Ota, and Erich Kulka. *The Death Factory: Document on Auschwitz.* Oxford, NY: Pergamon Press, 1966.

*Lengyel, Olga. *Five Chimneys: The Story of Auschwitz.* Chicago: Ziff-Davis, 1947.

*Levi, Primo. *Survival in Auschwitz: The Nazi Assault on Humanity.* New York: Simon & Schuster, 1958.

Menasche, Albert, Number 124,454. *Birkenau (Auschwitz II): Memories of an Eyewitness: How 72,000 Greek Jews Perished.* New York: I. Saltiel, 1947.

Müller, Filip. *Eyewitness Auschwitz: Three Years in the Gas Chambers.* New York: Stein and Day, 1979.

Nahon, Marco. *Birkenau: The Camp of Death.* Tuscaloosa: University of Alabama Press, 1989.

Shelley, Lore, ed. *Auschwitz — the Nazi Civilization: Twenty-three Women Prisoners' Accounts.* Lanham, MD: University Press of America, 1992.

———. *The Union Kommando in Auschwitz: The Auschwitz Munitions Factory Through the Eyes of Its Former Slave Laborers.* Lanham, MD: University Press of America, 1996.

"Like Thunder in the Spring"

Arad, Yitzhak. *Belzec, Sobibor, Treblinka: The Operation Reinhard Death Camps.* Bloomington: Indiana University Press, 1987.

*Blatt, Thomas Toivi. *From the Ashes of Sobibor: A Story of Survival.* Evanston, IL: Northwestern University Press, 1997.

———. "Sobibor: The Forgotten Revolt." http://www.sobibor.info.

*———. *Sobibor, the Forgotten Revolt: A Survivor's Report.* Issaquah, WA: H.E.P., 1997.

Glazar, Richard. *Trap with a Green Fence: Survival in Treblinka.* Evanston, IL: Northwestern University Press, 1995.

Novitch, Miriam. *Sobibór: Martyrdom and Revolt: Documents and Testimonies.* New York: Holocaust Library, 1980.

*Rashke, Richard. *Escape from Sobibor.* Urbana and Chicago: University of Illinois Press, 1995.

*Schelvis, Jules. *Sobibor: A History of a Nazi Death Camp.* Oxford, NY, and Washington, D.C.: Berg and the United States Holocaust Memorial Museum, 2007.

Sobibor Roll of Remembrance. http://www.deathcamps.org/sobibor.

Suhl, Yuri, ed. *They Fought Back: The Story of the Jewish Resistance in Nazi Europe.* New York: Schocken, 1967.

PART FIVE: PARTISAN WARFARE

"This song was written with our blood, and not with lead"

Kramer, Aaron, ed. *The Last Lullaby: Poetry from the Holocaust*. Syracuse, NY: Syracuse University Press, 1998.

Sabotage!

Same sources as for "A Wrenching Decision" (see pages 211–212), as well as the following:

Baum Memorial. http://fcit.usf.edu/holocaust/photos/berres/berres.htm.

Suhl, Yuri, ed. *They Fought Back: The Story of the Jewish Resistance in Nazi Europe*. New York: Schocken, 1967.

Wollheim Monument. www.wollheim-memorial.de.

Long Live the Resistance!

Latour, Anny. *Jewish Resistance in France, 1940–1944*. New York: Holocaust Library, 1981.

The Manouchian Group. http://www.marxists.org/history/france/resistance/manouchian/manouchian-group.htm.

Poznanski, Renée. *Jews in France During World War II*. Hanover, NH: Brandeis University Press/University Press of New England, in association with the United States Holocaust Memorial Museum, 2001.

Suhl, Yuri, ed. *They Fought Back: The Story of the Jewish Resistance in Nazi Europe*. New York: Schocken, 1967.

Invisible Warriors

Ben, Yosef. *Greek Jewry in the Holocaust and the Resistance, 1941–1944*. Tel Aviv: Institute of the Salonika Jewry Research Center, l985.

Benaroya, Avraam. "The Movement of Resistance of the Jews of Greece Against the German Oppression." In Memorium of Salonike (Thessaloniki, Greece). www.jewishgen.org/Yizkor/Thessalonika/thev/thev2_555.html.

*Bowman, Steven. *The Agony of Greek Jews, 1940–1945*. Stanford: Stanford University Press, 2009.

———. *Jewish Resistance in Wartime Greece*. London: Valentine Mitchell, 2006.

Cohen, Leon. *From Greece to Birkenau: The Crematoria Workers' Uprising*. Translated from the French by Jose-Maurice Gormezano. Tel-Aviv: Salonika Research Center, 1996.

Fromer, Rebecca Camhi. *The Holocaust Odyssey of Daniel Bennahmias, Sonderkommando.* Tuscaloosa: University of Alabama Press, 1993.

Jewish Partisan Educational Foundation. http://www.jewishpartisans.org.

Kabeli, Isaac. "Jews in Greek Insurrections." *JHI Bulletins* 36B (1953).

Kitroeff, Alexandros. "The Jews in Greece, 1941–1944: Eyewitness Accounts." *Journal of the Hellenic Diaspora* 12:3 (1985): pp. 5–32.

*Matsas, Michael. *The Illusion of Safety: The Story of the Greek Jews During the Second World War.* New York: Pella, 1997.

Mazower, Mark. *Inside Hitler's Greece: The Experience of Occupation, 1941–44.* New Haven: Yale University Press, 1993.

Melammed, Renée Levine. "The Memoirs of a Partisan from Salonika." *Nashim: A Journal of Jewish Women's Studies and Gender Issues* 7 (spring 2004): pp. 151–173.

Menasche, Albert. "The Resistance of the Greek Jews." *YIVO Annual of the Jewish Social Sciences* (1953): pp. 281–288.

Novitch, Miriam. *The Passage of the Barbarians (Jews in Wartime, 1939–1945).* Hull, England: Wilberforce Council, 1989.

The Violinist

Ainsztein, Reuben. *Jewish Resistance in Nazi-Occupied Eastern Europe.* New York: Barnes & Noble, 1975.

Arad, Yitzhak. *In the Shadow of the Red Banner: Soviet Jews in the War Against Nazi Germany.* Jerusalem: Gefen Publishing House, 2010.

Gerasimova, Inna, Viacheslav Selemenev, and Jack Kagan. *We Stood Shoulder to Shoulder: Jewish Partisans in Byelorussia, 1941–1944.* Bury St. Edmunds, Suffolk, England: Arima Publishing, 2010.

Suhl, Yuri, ed. *They Fought Back: The Story of the Jewish Resistance in Nazi Europe.* New York: Schocken, 1967.

"I am a Jew and will be a Jew forever"

Volavková, Hana, ed. *I Never Saw Another Another Butterfly: Children's Drawings and Poems from Terezin Concentration Camp, 1942–1944.* Prague: Jewish Museum; New York: Schocken, 1993.

PHOTOGRAPHY AND ART CREDITS

p. ii: © United States Holocaust Memorial Museum (USHMM), courtesy of Rina Elisha

pp. vi–vii, background: © USHMM, Stadtarchiv Hechingen/USHMM, courtesy of Dr. Adolf Vees

pp. viii–ix, background: National Archives and Records Administration, College Park, Maryland

p. 2: Heinrich Hoffmann/Studio of H. Hoffmann, © USHMM, courtesy of James Sander

pp. 2–3, background: © USHMM/Dokumentationsarchiv des Österreichischen Widerstandes

p. 3, upper right: © USHMM, courtesy of Hans Frankl; bottom right: Heinrich Hoffmann/Studio of H. Hoffmann, © USHMM, courtesy of Richard Freinmark and William O. McWorkman

p. 4: From the personal archive of Ernest Günter Fontheim

p. 5, background: Georg Schmidt, Trudy Isenberg Collection/USHMM, © USHMM

p. 6: © USHMM, Stadtarchiv Hechingen/USHMM, courtesy of Dr. Adolf Vees

p. 7: © USHMM

p. 8 and pp. 8–9, background: © USHMM/American Jewish Joint Distribution Committee (AJDC), courtesy of Robert A. Schmuhl

p. 9: © Yad Vashem, courtesy of Lester Hajenina

p. 11: Courtesy of Ilse Kessler (née Prager)

p. 12: Herbert Sonnenfeld, © Sonnenfeld Collection/Beth Hatefutsoth Photo Archive

p. 14: Sport and General Press Agency Ltd., © Instytut Pamięci Narodowej

p. 15: © USHMM, courtesy of Gerda Levy Lowenstein

p. 16: Herbert Sonnenfeld, © Sonnenfeld Collection/Beth Hatefutsoth Photo Archive

p. 18, map: Karen Minot, © Candlewick Press

pp. 18–19, background: Mensing, © Bundesarchiv

p. 19, top right: © Memorijalni muzej Jasenovac; left: © USHMM, courtesy of Charles and Hana Bruml; bottom right: © USHMM, courtesy of Claudine Cerf

p. 20: © Ghetto Fighters' House (GFH)

pp. 20–21, background: Mémorial de la Shoah/Centre de Documentation Juive Contemporaine (CDJC), © CDJC

p. 21: © GFH

p. 22: © Yad Vashem, courtesy of Yde Lang

p. 23, top: Lydia Riezouw, M. van Nobelen/Tollenstraat 199/1053 RV/Amsterdam, © Nederlands Instituut voor Oorlogsdocumentatie (NIOD); bottom: © USHMM, courtesy of Hilde Jacobsthal Goldberg

p. 24, both images: © USHMM, courtesy of Hilde Jacobsthal Goldberg

p. 26: Violet Cornelius, © Nederlands Fotomuseum

p. 27: © NIOD

p. 28, top: © GFH; middle, row left, second from left, and far right: © Yad Vashem, courtesy of Mirjam Waterman-Pinkhof; middle row, second from right: © GFH; bottom: © GFH

p. 29, top: © Kazerne Dossin — Fonds, Belgium; bottom: © USHMM

p. 30: © Yad Vashem, courtesy of Andrée Geulen Herscovici

p. 31, top: © USHMM, courtesy of Anne Marie Yellin; bottom: © USHMM, courtesy of Miriam Frydland Keyes

p. 32: © USHMM, courtesy of Andrée Geulen Herscovici

pp. 32–33, background: © Yad Vashem, courtesy of Andrée Geulen Herscovici

p. 33: © USHMM, courtesy of Myriam Frydland Keyes

p. 34: © Yad Vashem, courtesy of Moshe Shalvi

p. 36: Courtesy of Bernard Fenerberg

p. 37: © Mémorial de la Shoah/CDJC

p. 38, top: © USHMM, courtesy of Niomi Elath; bottom: © USHMM, courtesy of Lida Jablonski

p. 39: © USHMM, courtesy of Elaine Frank and Claudine Cerf

pp. 40–41, background: © USHMM

p. 44: © Yad Vashem, courtesy of Anciens de la Résistance Juive en France

p. 45, top: © Yad Vashem, courtesy of David Silberklang/DR. Ginat; bottom: © Guy Gavard

p. 46, both images: © Guy Gavard

p. 47, top: Wikipedia/public domain; bottom: © Yad Vashem, courtesy of Anciens de le Résistance Juive en France

p. 48: © Yad Vashem

pp. 48–49, background: © Bartlomiej Magierowski, Shutterstock

p. 49: © Yad Vashem, courtesy of Gefter Leonid

p. 50, top: © USHMM, courtesy of the Bielski family; bottom: © GFH

p. 51, both images: © GFH

pp. 52–53, background: Leizer Novitzky, © USHMM/Jack Lennard Archive/Yad Vashem Photo Archives, courtesy of Moshe Kaganovich

p. 55: © GFH

p. 57, map: Karen Minot, based on a diagram provided courtesy of Florida Holocaust Museum, © Candlewick Press

p. 58, top: © Yad Vashem; bottom: © USHMM, courtesy of the Bielski family

p. 60, top: © Yad Vashem, courtesy of Dr. Krakowski; bottom: Library of Congress/Dokumentationsarchiv des Österreichischen Widerstandes/USHMM/YIVO/Institute for Jewish Research, courtesy of Sharon Paquette

pp. 60–61, background: © Yad Vashem, courtesy of Dr. Krakowski

p. 61, top: © Dokumentationsarchiv des Österreichischen Widerstandes/Yad Vashem, courtesy of Judith Levin; bottom: Nachman Zonabend, © Yad Vashem, courtesy of Archiwum Gt. Komisi

p. 62: © USHMM, courtesy of Irving Milchberg/Jan Kostanski

pp. 62–63, background: © GFH

p. 63: © GFH

p. 64: © Yad Vashem, courtesy of Moshe Shalvi

p. 65, map: Karen Minot, © Candlewick Press

p. 66: © USHMM/Beit Lohamei Haghetaot, courtesy of Benjamin (Miedzyrzecki) Meed

p. 67: © GFH

p. 68: photograph © by the author, taken in the GFH Museum

p. 70, left: From an album assembled by SS major general Jürgen Stroop for "The Stroop Report," National Archives and Records Administration, College Park, Maryland/Instytut Pamięci Narodowej; right: National Archives and Records Administration, College Park, Maryland/Instytut Pamięci Narodowej

p. 71, background: From an album assembled by SS major general Jürgen Stroop for "The Stroop Report," © GFH

p. 72: National Archives and Records Administration, College Park, Maryland/USHMM, courtesy of Louis Gonda

p. 75: © Instytut Pamięci Narodowej/Yad Vashem

p. 76, top: © USHMM, courtesy of Benjamin (Miedzyrzecki) Meed; bottom: photograph by SS-PK or SS photographer, © Yad Vashem, courtesy of Genia Markun

p. 77: National Archives and Records Administration, College Park, Maryland/USHMM, courtesy of Louis Gonda

p. 78 and pp. 78–79, background: National Archives and Records Administration, College Park, Maryland/Instytut Pamięci Narodowej

p. 79, map: Karen Minot, © Candlewick Press

p. 80: © GFH

p. 81: © Yad Vashem

p. 82, top: © Yad Vashem/*Encyclopedia of the Holocaust* — Hebrew edition 1990, courtesy of Moshe Shalvi; bottom: © Yad Vashem, courtesy of Alexander Bernfas

p. 83: © USHMM, courtesy of Leopold Page Photographic Collection

p. 84, top: © GFH; bottom: © USHMM, courtesy of Shlomo Nadel

p. 85, background: © Yad Vashem, courtesy of Alexander Bernfas

p. 86, top: © Yad Vashem, courtesy of Alexander Bernfas; bottom: © Yad Vashem, courtesy of Deborah Richardson

p. 87, top: © USHMM, Lydia Chagoll Collection; bottom: Naomi Salmon, © Yad Vashem, courtesy of Chava Pressburger/Nina Shpringer Aharoni

pp. 88–89, background: Petr Ginz (1928–1944) *Dwellings in the Youth Barracks*, 1943, watercolor on paper, collection of the Yad Vashem Art Museum, Jerusalem, gift of Otto Ginz, Haifa; reproduced by permission

p. 89: Eva Nemcova, © Terezín Memorial Archives

pp. 90–91, all images: © Jewish Museum, Prague

pp. 92 and 93: © Jewish Museum, Prague

p. 94: © Yad Vashem, courtesy of Willi Dressen/Dr. Krakowski

p. 95, background: © Yad Vashem, courtesy of Nachum Alfret/Moshe Aloi; top: © Yad Vashem; bottom: © USHMM, courtesy of Vitka Kempner Kovner

pp. 96 and 97: © GFH

p. 98: © USHMM, courtesy of William Begell

p. 99: © Yad Vashem

p. 101: © Vilna Gaon State Jewish Museum

p. 102: © Yad Vashem, courtesy of Central Government Archives, Moscow/Dr. Krakowski

pp. 102–103, background: © Yad Vashem

p. 104: © GFH

p. 105: © Yad Vashem

p. 108: © USHMM, courtesy of Friedel Bohny-Reiter

pp. 108–109, background: © Yad Vashem

p. 109: © USHMM, courtesy of Hilda Tayar

pp. 110 and 111: © Kazerne Dossin — Fonds, Belgium

p. 113, top: © Yad Vashem; bottom left and right: © Kazerne Dossin — Fonds, Belgium

p. 114: © Kazerne Dossin — Fonds, Belgium

p. 116: © Kazerne Dossin — Fonds, Belgium

pp. 118–119, background: The Holocaust Museum Houston

p. 121: © Marc Michiels, Belgium

p. 122, top: National Archives and Records Administration, College Park, Maryland; bottom: Jewish Historical Museum, Belgrade

pp. 122–123, background and p. 123, bottom right: © USHMM/Instytut Pamięci Narodowej, courtesy of Leopold Page Photographic Collection

p. 123, top left: © USHMM, courtesy of George Kadish/Zvi Kadushin; top right: © USHMM, courtesy of Bella Rotner

p. 124: From the personal archives of Jack Kagan

p. 125, top: From the personal archives of Jack Kagan; bottom: © GFH

pp. 127–135: From the personal archives of Jack Kagan

p. 136, top: Unknown SS photographer, © Yad Vashem, courtesy of Otto Dov Kulka

pp. 136–137, background: © Instytut Pamięci Narodowej

p. 137: Bernhardt Walter/Ernst Hoffmann, © Yad Vashem

p. 138: From the personal archives of Israel Cohen

p. 139: © Yad Vashem

p. 141: National Archives and Records Administration, College Park, Maryland

p. 142: © Yad Vashem, courtesy of Ziva Noach

p. 143: © USHMM, courtesy of Henryk and Juta Bergman

p. 144, top: © USHMM, courtesy of Anna and Josh Heilman; bottom: © GFH

p. 145: Yad Vashem/Państwowe Muzeum Auschwitz-Birkenau w Oświęcimiu

p. 146, top: © Yad Vashem; bottom: © USHMM, courtesy of Anna and Joshua Heilman

pp. 146–147, background: © USHMM/American Red Cross/Yad Vashem Photo Archives/YIVO/Institute for Jewish Research, courtesy of Philip Vock

p. 147: Bernhardt Walter/Ernst Hofmann, Yad Vashem

p. 148, top: © Yad Vashem; bottom: © GFH

p. 151: Unknown SS photographer, © Yad Vashem, courtesy of Otto Dov Kulka

p. 152: © Yad Vashem, courtesy of Alice Schick

p. 153: © USHMM, courtesy of Anna and Joshua Heilman

p. 154: Bernahrdt Walter/Ernst Hofmann © Yad Vashem/Panstwowe Muzeum Auschwitz-Birkenau w Oświęcimiu

pp. 154–155, background: © Yad Vashem, courtesy of Bernfes Archives

p. 155, left: © Dokumentationsarchiv des Österreichischen Widerstandes; right: Sigmond Zumbacki, © Yad Vashem, courtesy of Frantishk Chonbecki

p. 156, top: © GFH; bottom: Wikipedia/public domain; background: © USHMM, courtesy of Polskie Koleje Pańtswowe S.A.

p. 157, both images: © GFH

p. 158: © Yad Vashem

p. 159: © GFH; background: © Yad Vashem

p. 160, background: © Yad Vashem

p. 161, diagram: Karen Minot, © Candlewick Press

p. 163: © Yad Vashem/Main Commission for the Investigation of Nazi War Crimes

p. 164: © Museum of Jewish Heritage

p. 166: © GFH; background: © Yad Vashem

p. 168: © Yad Vashem, courtesy of Beth Hatefutsoth

pp. 168–169, background: © Yad Vashem

p. 169, top: Faye Schulman (Faigel Lazebnik), Museum of the Great Patriotic War; bottom: © Yad Vashem, courtesy of Abrascha Arluk-Lawit/Dr. Arad

p. 170, top: Margot Pikarski, courtesy of Eric Brothers; bottom: SZ Photo/S.M./The Image Works

p. 171: © Bildarchiv Preeussischer Kulturbesitz/USHMM

pp. 172: top: © Reproduktion Gedenkstätte Deutscher Widerstand; bottom and pp. 172–173, background: From the personal collection of Randall Bytwerk, German Propaganda Archive, www.calvin.edu/cas/gpa

p. 174, both images: © Yad Vashem, courtesy of Moshe Shalvi

p. 176: © GFH

pp. 176–177, background: © Yad Vashem

p. 177, top left: © Yad Vashem, courtesy of David Silberklang/DR. Ginat; top right: © USHMM, courtesy of Arnold Einhorn; bottom: © GFH

p. 178, top: Jay Robert Nash Collection/CRIA Images; bottom: collection FNDIRP, France

p. 181: © Yad Vashem, courtesy of Tigran Drombian/Mark Goldman

p. 182 and pp. 182–183, background: © USHMM, courtesy of Jamila Kolonomos

p. 183, map: Karen Minot, © Candlewick Press

p. 184: Wetzel, © Bundesarchiv

pp. 185 and 186: © USHMM, courtesy of Yitzchak Kerem

p. 187: Jewish Partisan Educational Foundation

p. 188: © Yad Vashem, courtesy of Krosnokork Photo Archives, Moscow

p. 189, left: © GFH; right: © USHMM, courtesy of Dov Levin; background: © Yad Vashem

p. 190: © USHMM

pp. 192–193, background: © Yad Vashem, courtesy of Martynenko

p. 195: © Yad Vashem Artifacts Collection. Gift of Yousef (Seffi) Hanegbi, Arad and Zahava Shanni, Rechovot, Israel

INDEX

Page numbers in *italics* indicate caption text and/or illustrations.